Praise Her in the Gates

PRAISE HER
IN THE GATES

The Calling of Christian Motherhood

Nancy Wilson

canonpress
Moscow, Idaho

Published by Canon Press
P.O. Box 8729, Moscow, ID 83843
800-488-2034 | www.canonpress.com

Nancy Wilson, *Praise Her in the Gates:
The Calling of Christian Motherhood*
Copyright © 2000 by Nancy Wilson

Cover design by Paige Atwood.
Printed in the United States of America.

Library of Congress Cataloging-in-Publication Data

Wilson, Nancy
  Praise her in the gates : the calling of Christian motherhood / Nancy Wilson.
    p. cm.
  ISBN-13: 978-1-885767-70-7
  ISBN-10: 1-885767-70-6
  1. Motherhood—Religious aspects—Christianity. 2. Christian women—Religious life. I. Title.
    BV4529.18 .W56 2000
    248.8'431—dc21
                                    00-009453

10 11 12 13 14 15 16 17 18   11 10 9 8 7 6

To my parents for their wisdom,
my children for their joy,
my grandchildren for their promise.

Contents

CHAPTER ONE

The Big Picture

> And in you all the families of the earth shall
> be blessed. (Gen. 12:3)

Today the Church is characterized by much confusion about
the role of the mother. What the Scriptures teach so plainly
and simply is twisted beyond recognition by those who
refuse to submit to God's Word. The world has infiltrated
the Church and is leading women astray, teaching them to
dismiss the biblical pattern for motherhood. But as God mer-
cifully grants reformation and revival to His Church, many
families are discovering that they have been either duped
or disobedient, and many are returning to the old paths
laid out in Scripture. It is essential that Christian mothers
understand their calling so that they can whole-heartedly
embrace it. When mothers faithfully obey God in this very
precious and demanding role, they can expect God to fulfill
His promise of blessing in their families.

As I discuss the mother's calling in this book, I will
examine different challenging aspects of the mother's duties
in the home, from childbirth to the time when the children
leave home. But before discussing these specific areas, it is
important to look at the big picture. Anytime we take on an
important job, it is very helpful if we have a vision for the
end result. If you are building a home, you may not be able
to see with your eyes what the final product will be, but you
can, by faith so to speak, know what you are shooting for.
The house plans lay out the complete design, and as each wall

goes up, it should follow this master plan. Because mothering is very similar, a mother needs to see her daily tasks in light of the whole design. Each day's work is significant, for it is contributing toward the long-term plan. Though we may be tempted to think that this particular nail in this particular stud wall will not make much difference in the way the home looks in the end, a wise builder knows better. Each nail is important and ensures that the house will stand and not topple over in the first storm. Mothers must see each day's duties as part of this building process. Though it may not seem like much got accomplished in a single day, all those nails in the walls do add up. "The wise woman builds her house, but the foolish pulls it down with her hands" (Prov. 14:1).

Let's turn now to see what the Scriptures say about this master plan and why the mother's calling is so significant. First we will consider the positive biblical images of motherhood from Psalms and Proverbs, and then we will look at specific instructions to mothers in the New Testament.

Psalm 127 and 128 are often cited for their beautiful imagery describing mothers and children in the home. In Psalm 127 children are called a "heritage from the Lord," a "reward," and compared to "arrows in the hand of a warrior." The man with a full quiver is happy because his children give him stature in the community as a sign of the Lord's blessing. The virtuous wife in Proverbs 31 has succeeded in her duties because "her children rise up and call her blessed." The fruit of her hands praise her in the gates, her husband and her children testify to her obedience in her calling, and she is commended for this fruitful obedience.

Consider the lovely images of Psalm 128. Blessings for the one who fears God include happiness around the dinner table where the fruit of hard labor is enjoyed. The wife is described as a fruitful vine. And where is she? "In the very heart of your house." The mother is central to the picture of blessing and prosperity. Around the table are the olive shoots, an image of promise and growth and future prosperity. This psalm concludes with a blessing: "Yes, may you see your children's children. Peace be upon Israel!" A mother who fulfills her fruitful calling is a means God uses to bring blessing for her entire family, her husband, the church, and the community.

Mothers who understand that God desires "godly offspring" (Mal. 2:15) realize what an important part they play in fulfilling God's desire. It takes diligence, hard work, and faith to raise godly offspring for God, but it is a soul-satisfying work. This biblical view of a God-fearing motherhood is one laden with images of fruit and abounding in spiritual excellence and honor and blessing. The woman described in Proverbs 31 is a satisfied woman. She can look with pleasure on her years of hard work raising children and managing her household. She reaps a harvest of good things from her hard work of sowing obedience. This is the house reaching the final stages of completion. The mother of young children must have an eye toward the day when all her children, by the grace of God, will be adults who rise up in her presence and bless her. It may be difficult to maintain this long view in the midst of diapers and discipline and schooling and a hundred other things. But the Christian mother must look to see the house finished. Her obedience is central in passing on to her children a love for the Most High God. He is faithful and He has promised our children to us. Mothers must be faithful in trusting their children to Him.

Now let's consider Titus 2:4-5. This passage assigns duties to the women in the church. The older women are to be teachers, instructing the younger women. The younger women are to be learners, applying this teaching. What is it the older women are to teach? "That they may teach the young women to be sober, to love their husbands, to love their children, to be discreet, chaste, keepers at home, good, obedient to their own husbands, that the word of God be not blasphemed." This good teaching enables the mother to flourish and excel in her duties in the home, and it enables her to have a tremendous impact on her family. As the older women pass on their good teaching, the whole Christian community is blessed. The young mothers can turn to the older women for help, support, teaching, and encouragement; meanwhile, the older women have a vital role in the Church and need not be on the periphery, but rather they should be busy fulfilling their calling of passing on mothering (as well as home-keeping) skills to the next generation of mothers.

Finally, we must consider what happens when mothers are fulfilling their God-given calling in the home. When women devote themselves to their husbands, children, and to building their house, the whole Church is strengthened. This is actually their "ministry" to the Church: being obedient wives who are raising godly children. Obviously, when a church is full of healthy families, the Church will be healthy and stable.

When mothers see how valuable their contribution can be, they should be overwhelmed with gratitude to God for bestowing such good work upon them. Making a home is a good work. As we shall see in the following chapters, raising children is a good work.

CHAPTER TWO

The Church Our Mother

> But Jerusalem which is above is free, which is the
> mother of us all. For it is written, Rejoice, thou barren
> that bearest not; break forth and cry, thou that travail-
> est not: for the desolate hath many more children than
> she which hath an husband. (Gal. 4:26-27)

When men assume the role of husband and father, the scriptural paradigm they follow is that of God the Father (Eph.
3:14-15) and Christ the Bridegroom (Eph. 5:25). They have
a masculine paradigm to follow and must imitate Christ
as they love their brides as Christ loves the Church. Wives
also have a scriptural paradigm to follow, for they are commanded to imitate the Church. "Therefore as the church is
subject unto Christ, so let wives be to their own husbands
in everything" (Eph. 5:24).

The Christian Church is called the new Jerusalem and a
bride: "And I John saw the holy city, new Jerusalem, coming
down from God out of heaven, prepared as a bride adorned
for her husband" (Rev. 21:2). In verse nine, the Church is
similarly called, "the bride, the Lamb's wife." Clearly, the
Church is the model for earthly brides.

This bridal model is also maternal. Galatians 4:21-27
explains the allegory of the two covenants, and it identifies
the new Jerusalem as "the mother of us all." In this modern
day when the Church has abandoned its duties and roles, it
may be difficult for us to see our duties as mothers as they
are pictured for us in the Church. Sadly, vast numbers of

mothers today (in the Church, as well as in the world) have abandoned or murdered their own children. But they learned this first from the Church, when the Church ceased to teach the truth, failed to correct and discipline its members, and rejected its commission of fruit bearing and nurturing to pursue its own entertainment and pleasure. Nevertheless, let's examine the Church's God-ordained duties that mothers can follow as their scriptural and maternal paradigm.

All the Church's responsibilities are commanded by God, and the Church is to submit joyfully to Christ; in the same way, a mother's duties are laid out in Scripture and are delegated to her by her husband. When God gives a commandment, He also provides the grace to do it. In all their responsibilities in childrearing, wives must look to their husbands and "submit yourselves unto your own husbands, as it is fit in the Lord" (Col. 3:18). This means that wives are not any more autonomous than the Church is; a wife must look to her head as the Church looks to Christ. "For the husband is the head of the wife, even as Christ is the head of the church: and he is the saviour of the body. Therefore as the church is subject unto Christ, so let the wives be to their own husbands in everything" (Eph. 5:23-24).

When a wife lurches off to do what she thinks is her responsibility without her husband's blessing and delegation, she is out of bounds and unprotected. In the case of a single mom or a wife of an abdicating husband, she must look for the Lord's blessing and protection by being careful and wise about her duties and her manner of fulfilling them, and she must look for pastoral help in these things. Just as the Church today is doing many things that seem like a "good idea," if they are not mandated by Scripture, the Church is out of bounds, disobedient, and unprotected. Wise women will not imitate a disobedient Church. So as we go over these duties that are modeled for us by the obedient Church, we must remember that our submission to our husbands is a necessary foundation for our obedience and success in our duties. And in examining what we can learn of some of our duties, I am not negating the father's obvious duties in these same areas. Fathers are to take responsibility, provide, and protect, but this does not mean they have no part of teaching, nourishing, disciplining, etc. Nevertheless, it is my purpose here to examine a mother's duties as she imitates the Church.

The Church is responsible to teach and build up. This is an obvious duty of mothers. We are to teach the children God graciously gives us from the moment they arrive in our home. We are not responsible to teach the neighbor's kids; we are responsible for our own, and that means all of them. We cannot let any "slip through the cracks" because they came when our hands were full. If God blesses a household with many children, just as He blesses some churches with many members, it is no excuse to say that there were just too many to teach. A mother is responsible to know how her children are doing, how they are learning, and see to it that each one is being built up, prospering under her teaching. This does not mean that she can never delegate, as many do when they send their children to a Christian school. Just as the pastor of the church does not have to do all the teaching, but others appointed by the church can help in the teaching, so a mother can delegate teaching to a qualified individual or school for the same purpose. She must insure that the teaching her children receive, whether directly from her or from others, is indeed the sort that builds up and does not tear down.

The Church is appointed to feed and nourish the flock. This is closely related to the duty of teaching and building up but includes spiritual food and nourishment. A mother must see that her children know they are loved, for they must be nourished by mother's love. A newborn is fed at the mother's breast, and this is a lovely picture of how the Church is to feed us. The milk a baby receives at the breast is not only nourishing physically, it is emotionally nourishing. Mother is close, not across the room. When Mother sings and rocks and holds her little ones, she is feeding and nourishing in soul-prospering ways. And not only are her children blessed, she is also. Scripture says it is more blessed to give than receive, and this is certainly true in the area of mothering. One of the benefits of breast-feeding is the necessity of sitting down, holding the child close, and putting aside all distractions. It is a time for communion with the child and a time to reflect on the mystery of this heavenly gift of the breast. How do we produce this milk anyway? God does and it is a marvel. How does the preaching of the Word nourish God's people who sit under the teaching with attentiveness? Do we do it? Certainly not. God does and it is a marvel. Oh, that we would be as attentive to the Word as a newborn is to the milk.

Next, the Church disciplines and corrects its own. In fact, discipline is a sign of a family connection: "For whom the Lord loveth he chasteneth, and scourgeth every son whom he receiveth. If ye endure chastening, God dealeth with you as with sons; for what son is he whom the father chasteneth not? But if ye be without chastisement, whereof all are partakers, then are ye bastards, and not sons?" (Heb. 12:6-8). Mothers are responsible to discipline and correct their children. Because mothers are in the home with the children, much correction will necessarily come from Mom. Of course there will be times when she will need her head to step in to give input, provide wisdom and direction, and even to administer the correction. But mothers must not abdicate and assume father will take care of it all when he gets home. Correction must be judicial, kind, and loving, even when it is painful, and it must be done promptly and consistently. This is an enormous task, but when it is faithfully carried out, the children are healthy and happy. When the Church disciplines biblically, the whole body is healthy in the same way. When discipline is forsaken and sin is indulged, no one is happy, and the church or the family is overrun with sin and all its consequences of misery and joylessness. Mothers must be careful to guard their own hearts as they discipline. In *The Quest for Meekness and Quietness of Spirit*, Matthew Henry puts it this way: "But while you are governing others, learn to govern yourselves, and do not disorder your own souls under the pretense of keeping order in your families."

Finally, the Church is fruitful. While evangelism brings more worshipers into the Church, childbearing brings more disciples into the home. A mother should be fruitful like the vine in Psalm 128. Children are not to be viewed as a hindrance, an intrusion, an interruption, or a burden. Fruit is not viewed in such a way. Of course fruit requires tending, and tending can be hard work. But it is good work. Women should see that their view of children is shaped by Scripture and not by the world. Hard work, when it is good work, is soul-satisfying and soul-prospering. No matter how many children the Lord may give you, be it two or twelve, you must rejoice in the number and be fruitful in the rearing of them. The Church becomes barren when it is disobedient. Women today embrace barrenness as freedom, and yet barrenness is always a curse in Scripture. But fruitfulness includes more than just childbearing; it is descriptive of a lifestyle. "For if these things are yours and abound, you will be neither barren nor unfruitful in the knowledge of our Lord Jesus Christ" (2 Pet. 1:8).

CHAPTER THREE

Conception, Pregnancy, Childbirth

> For thou hast possessed my reins; thou hast covered
> me in my mother's womb. (Ps. 39:13)

When women talk about babies, they are talking shop. It is
only natural that they develop strong opinions about nearly
everything having to do with conception, pregnancy, childbirth, and child care. At the same time, it is only natural that
many old wives' tales surround these womanly subjects.
Old wives' tales may be around for generations, but they
are foolish by nature. Even in Paul's day he had to caution
Timothy to "reject profane and old wives' fables, and exercise
yourself toward godliness" (1 Tim. 4:7). In the first chapter,
Paul says not to "give heed to fables" because they "cause
disputes rather than godly edification which is in faith" (v.
4). In 2 Timothy 4:4, Paul describes those who "turn their
ears away from the truth" and are "turned aside to fables."
Now certainly Paul may not have had in mind fables about
childbirth, but nevertheless, the principle applies to all kinds
of falsehoods. When women have strong opinions about the
many issues surrounding the bearing and rearing of children,
they can cause division and disputation in the church. This
should not be.

We think of an old wives' tale as a silly story or supersti-
tious belief passed around by gossipy old women. Certainly
Christian women do not want to be characterized as listening to, believing in, or passing on silly stories as though
they were true. The fact they are named after old wives is

a sad statement on the general behavior of some women. Women can be easily deceived (1 Tim. 2:14) and can learn to be "not only idle but also gossips and busybodies, saying things which they ought not" (1 Tim. 5:13) and probably believing things they ought not. None of this is very flattering to women, but if we want to identify our temptations, we must listen to God's warnings to us through Paul. We must learn to separate truth from fiction when it comes to all we hear, read, or say about any subject, but especially (since this is our topic here) regarding our calling as wives and mothers. As we approach this subject, let us lay all our prejudices and favorite little pet notions aside and examine God's Word with a submissive spirit. Anyone can promote a pet theory by telling testimonies of amazing cures. This is an old device of propaganda. Even "facts" can be misleading. One "study" comes up with one conclusion to support its thesis while another "study" produces far different results. This calls for wisdom.

God commanded fruitfulness in Genesis before the fall. "Be fruitful and multiply; fill the earth and subdue it" (Gen. 1:28). Man and woman were given the joyful task of taking dominion over all the earth. But after the fall, God cursed the man in his calling and cursed the woman in *her* calling as a mother and as a wife: "I will greatly multiply your sorrow and your conception; in pain you shall bring forth children; your desire shall be for your husband, and he shall rule over you" (Gen. 3:16). Paul points out in 1 Timothy 2:15 that women can be saved in their calling: "Nevertheless she will be saved in childbearing if they continue in faith, love, and holiness, with self-control." God will call women to Himself as they are fulfilling their calling as wives and mothers.

Let's now turn and consider what the Bible says about conception, pregnancy, and childbirth. Then we will examine some of the old wives' tales surrounding these aspects of a woman's calling and discuss how we can discern between truth and falsehood and be self-controlled.

We know that children are from the Lord. They are His reward, His heritage, and He is the One who opens and closes the womb. When Eve gave birth to the first child, Cain, she said, "I have acquired a man from the Lord." When Cain killed his brother, Eve conceived again and bore Seth, saying, "For God has appointed another seed for me instead of Abel, whom Cain killed" (Gen. 4:25). This is evident also in Genesis 29:31: "When the Lord saw that Leah was unloved, He opened her womb; but Rachel was barren." And again in Genesis 30:22: "Then God remembered Rachel, and God listened to her and opened her womb." We learn in 1 Samuel 1:6 that Hannah was barren "because the Lord had closed her womb." There is no question that the Bible teaches that conception is controlled by the Almighty. Children are fruit and seed from God.

One form of "old wives' tale" that can accompany conception is attributing motives to God. If a woman cannot conceive or has a miscarriage, we ought not try to figure out *why* God is doing what He is doing. In the case of Leah, Scripture tells us why God gave her a child. But in our own cases, we do not have a word from Him telling us why things happen the way they do. We must trust in His kindness and sovereignty and know that He works everything for good for His children. After a miscarriage, a woman can worry that God may be punishing her for her sins. Of course we are all sinners, so we can always say that. But remember the blind man in the gospels. The Pharisees asked Jesus if his blindness was the result of his sin or his parents' sin. Jesus pointed out that it was neither. We must receive all from the hand of the Lord, and we can know it is for our ultimate good, without attaching specific motives to God.

We also know that God forms the child in the womb. "Did not the same One fashion us in the womb?" (Job 31:15). "For you formed my inward parts; you covered me in my mother's womb" (Ps. 139:13). And again in Isaiah 44:2, "Thus says the Lord who made you and formed you from the womb." A child is a marvelous work of God, as the psalmist says, "I will praise You, for I am fearfully and wonderfully made" (139:14).

It is the Lord who not only opens the womb, but He brings forth children from the womb. Job said, "Why then have You brought me out of the womb?" (Job 10:18). "You are He who took me out of the womb" (Ps. 71:6). Conception, pregnancy, and delivery are all of the Lord. Christian women must have this biblical truth thoroughly understood as foundational to all their thinking about their calling as mothers. We cannot play God when it comes to planning conception, pregnancy, or delivery. It is all of God's doing. We must be humble when we consider what He ordains to do in and through our bodies, and we must look to God for His sustaining grace through all aspects of this wonderful and awesome experience.

God has ordained pain in childbirth. "Rachel labored in childbirth, and she had a hard labor" (Gen. 35:16). Rachel not only had a hard labor, she died in childbirth. Childbirth has always been a dangerous work. It is no accident that the words *labor* and *delivery* are used. Just as men labor in the field, women labor in childbirth. It is *hard* work. *Pain* is not a bad word; at least the Scripture doesn't shy away from using it. The pain of childbirth is used as a comparison when describing God's judgment coming on a people. "They will be in pain as a woman in childbirth" (Is. 13:8). "Anguish has taken hold of him, pangs as of a woman in childbirth" (Jer. 50:43). "The sorrows of a woman in childbirth shall come upon him" (Hos. 13:13). When my husband was reading Anne Bradstreet's poem (cited below) at our annual American history conference, he introduced it by saying, "This is a woman preparing for battle." A woman certainly does have to prepare herself for labor and delivery much as a warrior prepares himself for war. This is a good work that women do, and it is a difficult and sometimes perilous engagement.

Christian women must realize that though childbearing has a blessed result, it is still a fallen and cursed process. It is not man who has made it a cursed process but God Himself. We cannot fool ourselves into thinking that we can make it easy or painless. Of course pregnancy is not a disease, but it is difficult. Yes, it is a natural or normal process, but it is still a cursed process, fraught with difficulty and even danger. To pretend that childbirth can be simple or to assume it will be a picnic is to believe an old wives' tale. Of course we should prepare for childbirth and do all we can to make it as successful and comfortable as possible, but we cannot deny that God has ordained pain in childbirth as a result of the fall. This runs counter to much non-Christian thinking. My point here is that all our preparations should be done before the Lord, acknowledging His sovereign hand over all these things and submitting to Him in childbirth as well as every other aspect of our lives. He gives us grace in our time of need, and delivering a child is a time of great need. Our preparations should be thorough; we should prepare both mentally and physically. We ought not think, "Since God is in control, there is nothing I can do." That is nonsense. God ordains both the end and the means. We should learn all we can to make the birthing process a triumph, knowing that we work out what God works in.

In centuries past, women commonly died in childbirth and babies also suffered a high mortality rate. Modern American women have much to be grateful for in this area. Few of us today are concerned that we may die in childbirth. It is truly rare. Consider this excerpt from a poem by Anne Bradstreet, the Puritan poet. She wrote this to her husband and called it "Before the birth of one of her children."

> How soon, my Dear, death may my steps attend,
> How soon't may be thy lot to lose thy friend.

The low mortality in childbirth in this country is God's goodness to us. He has provided much to us in the way of knowledge about pregnancy and childbirth, and women and babies can receive exceptional care when their lives are in danger. As Christians, there is no need for us to reject His gifts. Rather, we should cultivate gratitude.

At the same time, doctors in our country bear the guilt for the slaughter of thirty-seven million children over the past twenty-five years. We cannot entrust the care of our children to men and women who do not fear God and who murder babies in the womb. Although God is the One who has allowed us to find treatments for diseases, unregenerate man twists God's gifts and uses them for his own selfish ends. Certainly if all doctors did abortions, we would have to reject the profession all together. But there are many Christian nurses and doctors who can be trusted to help us take care of our children. To reject all of modern medicine because of the widespread wickedness would be foolish and believing an old wives' tale. In our community we are blessed with several Christian physicians and many Christian nurses who not only reject abortion but combine their training with a sincere desire to please and serve God while caring for people. These are the kind of physicians we should seek out, pray for, and thank God for. To lump all doctors together would not only be unkind to those with true integrity and faith, it would be a false representation and qualify as a fable.

Today with the rise of midwifery among Christians, many women are choosing to have their babies at home, and many with great success. Christian women must be very careful not to allow disputes over the choice of doctor versus midwife. Because women tend to feel strongly about these subjects, it is tempting to become imperialistic about their preferences, finding a Bible verse to supposedly support their view. We ought not try to proselytize women to our preference. This can nurture a "true believer" mentality that clutches at its own cause. Remember that word of mouth is not a reliable source of information. Do your own research. And women must be very careful to wait to be invited before giving their opinion. When we differ with one another over whether it is best to have babies in the hospital or at home, it is a thing "indifferent," at least as far as fellowship is concerned. We must not listen to those who use scare tactics to convince us of their view.

When a midwife says (as one said to my daughter), "If you go to the hospital they will shoot you full of drugs and stick you in a corner," you ought to be alert to the fact that she is either making a wild statement or you need to find out what hospital she is referring to and stay far away from it. This may be passing on old wives' tales. We live in a small town and our hospital has a good reputation. I had three children there, and I never had drugs, and I was never stuck in a corner. The truth is that many women *want* drugs and *ask* or even *beg* for drugs. Some of them are very grateful for drugs because in their case, drugs were a great blessing. That is an entirely different thing than "being shot full" of them. The Christian doctors I know do not *push* drugs, nor do they leave their patients in a corner.

Now of course the converse is true also. If a local midwife with a good reputation is being slandered, we ought not listen or pass it on. Midwives and doctors should be held to the same standard. There are well-trained, God-fearing midwives, as well as poorly trained, God-fearing midwives. We cannot lump them all together. (And of course, there is the other category of God-hating midwives; I am not even speaking here about them.) If fables are being passed around regarding midwifery, we ought to oppose them, whether we are personally supportive of midwifery or not. Fables are never to be used to support or refute our positions. The point is to have charity toward one another, even if we think we see a sister making what we believe to be a grievous mistake. I have seen the saints in our community rally around and help people in difficult circumstances, even if they disagreed with their medical decisions that got them into the difficulty. This is what Christian charity is.

The only way that fables can cause division is if they are pressed on women as gospel truth and a response is demanded. Some say that biblical modesty prohibits the presence of a male doctor at a birth. These same women, however, do not have the same convictions on the modesty issue when it comes to gynecological surgery. Some of these ideas are not from the Bible but are born of a male-hating feminism. Of course, all things being equal, it would be ideal to have women delivering babies. But all things are not equal. Women should not be so quick to criticize male doctors ("They all just want to cut you open so they can get back to their golf game") while overlooking all faults in female physicians or midwives. This is one of the signs of the "true believer" mentality. If a midwife is incompetent, those women who are supportive of midwifery ought to be the first to say so and not the first to overlook it. They should hold midwives accountable just as the community and the hospital hold doctors accountable. A poor midwife should not be recommended because she is a midwife any more than a poor doctor ought to be recommended.

Oftentimes midwifery is promoted by those who also embrace new-age philosophy. The Christian should stay away from all forms of such paganism. We should reject those unbelieving midwives who push their anti-medicine or anti-male philosophy on the Christian mother. In the same way, we should reject any unbelieving doctors who push their humanistic, God-hating philosophy of birth control or childrearing on women.

Our culture is obsessed with looking for the ultimate "experience." Childbirth is not always a wonderful experience. As I said above, Scripture teaches us that it is a fallen and cursed process with a blessed end. Some births are more difficult than others. Christian women must remember that a safe delivery, safe for both mother and child, is the objective under the blessing of God. A good "experience" is not the ultimate goal, although it is certainly to be desired and prayed for; all that we can do to prepare ought to be done. But when a woman has a difficult or hard experience, she ought not get bitter. Much of what you can hear or read promoting midwifery is tainted with bitterness toward doctors, hospitals, or medicine in general. Christian women need to remember that the sovereign God rules over all our experiences, good and bad, and He works them all for our good. We must not allow ourselves to become bitter toward anything or anyone. At the same time, we should make decisions based on what we know, without bitterness. If a midwife or hospital was inconsiderate or inept, we ought to go elsewhere for future deliveries, but not out of bitterness or resentment. This is sin, and certainly clouds our ability to reason. Stay away from bitter people who delight in telling their horror stories with an unforgiving, bitter tone. "Pursue peace with all people, and holiness, without which no one will see the Lord; looking carefully lest anyone fall short of the grace of God; lest any root of bitterness springing up cause trouble, and by this many become defiled" (Heb. 12:14-15). Bitterness is antithetical to peace: it causes trouble and defiles all who come into contact with it. Women who become bitter over childbirth experiences can spread their bitterness, infecting and defiling many others. Beware of such bitter roots and pursue peace and holiness. Our decisions should never be made out of fear, but rather before the Lord in faith and righteousness.

As I mentioned, our church community has a few godly Christian doctors who fear God and are proficient in delivering babies. These men are fathers themselves and have a high view of children and a high view of mothers. Not every community is equally blessed. Years ago one doctor in our town did abortions. For years many Christians prayed, marched, and wrote letters opposing abortion. Finally, he quit performing abortions. Today, three Christian doctors practice there and have prayer meetings once a week together. God answered our prayers far better than we ever expected.

And what about the women in the covenant community who are barren? As 2 Peter 1:8 states, all of us, with children or without, can "be neither barren nor unfruitful in the knowledge of our Lord Jesus Christ." And as the preceding two verses point out, God can enable women to be fruitful in their faith, in virtue, knowledge, self-control, perseverance, godliness, and kindness. Bearing and raising children is one kind of fruitfulness, but there are others. The instructions in Titus tell the older women to teach the younger women (as my husband likes to translate it) to be "into husbands" and "into kids."

A childless woman can still be "into kids" in many ways. She can visit women with young children, take care of children when their mother is sick, read to the children on one afternoon a week (as a friend of mine did for several summers), have them to her home for a picnic, teach them at a Christian school, or help out with homeschooling. Basically, she can get to know and love and enjoy many of the children in the church without actually being their mother. Fruitfulness includes extending hospitality, visiting the sick, helping the elderly, or a host of volunteer activities through the church or community. Fruitfulness is not limited to childbearing alone; if it was, we would all cease being fruitful when our children are grown. The Christian home should be a fruitful place, just as the Church should be. God is the One who gives the growth; it is our duty to obediently plant and water and pray for much fruit.

Obviously, much can be said about the subject of childbearing, and we all have much to learn about this marvelous process. May we learn to think biblically about every area of life, but particularly in this one that is so connected with who we are as women.

CHAPTER FOUR

When the Kids are Sick

> Blessed be God, even the Father of our Lord Jesus
> Christ, the Father of mercies, and the God of all
> comfort. (2 Cor. 1:4)

No mother wants to plan on her children being sick, and
yet it is a rare household that does not sometimes have sick
children. One of the obvious duties of a mother is to care for
her children when they are ill, and this can be short-term or
long-term, depending on the circumstances.

Perhaps the first thing to address is the tendency of
mothers to overreact. Our children are the Lord's, and they
are in His hands from beginning to end. We must trust our
children to His sovereign care and not be anxious about
them. He is the lender, and we are the borrowers. When our
children are sick, it is a good opportunity for us to exercise
our faith. Do we really believe God is in control of all things
and will work all things for our good, or do we just say this?
Sickness is a time when God tests us to see if we do really
believe He is good. When a child is ill, we must use discre-
tion and wisdom to determine how to care for him. Should
we call a doctor? Should we ride it out until morning? These
things call for wisdom and no decision should be made out
of panic or anxiety and fear. We must keep reason on the
throne when our emotions are being unruly. We must call
them into order and make a rational, thoughtful decision.

The other side of the coin is the tendency to under react.
This comes when a mother underestimates the seriousness

of the illness. A mother who is busy with many children may be tempted to assume that this illness can be treated with lots of Kleenex and some more vitamin C, when she should be far more concerned about the child. This attitude doesn't spring from anxiety, so she may feel superior to those "anxious mothers" who jump about every little cold. But her problem may be laziness, distraction, a desire not to be "bothered" by the time and expense of trips to the doctor, or a know-it-all attitude. This is the mother who sends her child to school or to the nursery at church with a runny nose and a terrible cough. She is not only inconsiderately exposing other children to the illness, but she is overlooking her child's misery so that her plans will not be interrupted by her child's untimely illness. When you feel crummy, you ought to be home. This is simply the golden rule when you apply it to your child. Sick children do interrupt our plans; that is what they are supposed to do. And we are to be interrupted cheerfully, even if it means missing church.

When my children were small, I often had to miss church because one or more of the kids were suffering from an ear infection or the croup or some other childhood sickness. One time a college student asked me where I went to church, assuming that my husband pastored one church while I attended another. (I didn't miss church *that* often.) But my point is this: what pleases God more? A woman home cheerfully taking care of her sick children and missing the worship service, or a woman with sick children who are suffering through the service, spreading their germs freely about the congregation? I think the answer is obvious.

In the church today alternative medicine is becoming a fascination with many people. This is an understandable reaction to the high costs of insurance and medical treatment and other factors that I have mentioned elsewhere. The decision you make as a family regarding these issues should not be made in the midst of an illness, but should be based on biblical principles and result from common sense and rational deliberation.

When women make medical decisions based on "statistics" that come to them word of mouth, they are being foolish. For example, consider the whole question of immunizations. It is true that some (very few) babies immunized contract the disease. No matter what the percentage is, when it is your baby, it is one out of one. At the same time, Christians ought to be advocates of good science, because it is a means of taking godly dominion. We ought not make our decisions out of fear. We do not want to become complacent and forget to thank God for His mercies brought to us through science. We should make decisions regarding health care for our children before the Lord. Women should discuss these things with their husbands and make decisions as a family. We should not be swayed by what we heard over coffee that frightened us, but rather we should think carefully about all we do while we trust God to protect us and lead us. If someone tells you a horror story about a child who contracted the disease and died from an immunization, remember there are also stories of children (many more in fact) of children who contracted the disease and died when an immunization would have protected them.

The whole debate over antibiotics is in this same category. We do not want to react against modern science; we want to use it to glorify God. Common sense tells us we should not take antibiotics as though they were candy. However, antibiotics can be a tremendous blessing in many, many cases. Countless lives are saved because of antibiotics. We must look for a balanced view in all things. We should not refuse what God has graciously given to us for our preservation. Fear should never be our motivation to reject or embrace anything. We fear God, not man nor his inventions. Christians, of all people, should see science as under God's sovereign control. And when the ungodly take God's good gifts and twist them to wicked ends, of course we should oppose and resist them.

When children are ill, it is a wonderful opportunity for teaching. You can model patience and cheerfulness to them when you get up in the night to comfort and minister to them. One of my daughter's happy memories is when she was sick with a respiratory illness. We sat in the bathroom in the wee hours of the night reading stories (*Chatterer the Red Squirrel*, in fact) and drinking pop while the shower steam helped her breathing. Mothers do have the capacity to make illness a happy memory. I remember my mother teaching me to braid with fat yarn when I was down with the chicken pox or some other illness. One spring break all three of our children fell ill the same day and were sick for the whole week. They still laugh about that "vacation" they spent in sleeping bags on the living room floor, watching old movies together and passing the Kleenex box around.

If mothers are worried, it will show. We must teach our children to trust God in their illnesses. If they are in too much pain to play *Sorry* or cards, we can give them back rubs, read to them, sing to them, cool their forehead with a washcloth, etc. Sometimes just being there in the room is all that you can do, and yet it is a tremendous comfort to your child. When they see you being calm, they will be too. Sickness is a good time to teach them about compassion and mercy, as well as about the frailty of life. Use all these times for spiritual profit.

When you go to a physician, try to find a Christian if you can. None of us wants our children to be quizzed behind our backs, nor do we want to be accused of child abuse if our child has fallen and has a black eye. We must be wise as serpents and innocent as doves. No matter what your views on medicine, there may be times when the emergency room is an absolute necessity. Keep your wits about you and do not leave your child for a minute unless it is for surgery. This is *your* child and you do not have to follow along blindly. It is very important that you have a physician that you know and trust and that you pray for this man or woman regularly. Your family should develop a relationship with him so he knows you.

Finally, if you have a child with a long-term illness, you will need long-term patience, resources, and stamina. You have a special burden in your home that the Lord has placed there for His own good purposes. Thank God for this child and his needs. Expect God to bless the entire household through this little person. I have seen wonderful Christian homes where the child with the special needs has been the source of tremendous spiritual growth and fruit for the whole family. The children learn to give and love in ways they never would have; the parents become people of great faith and are specially equipped to encourage and minister to others because of the child God placed in their home.

In all questions regarding medical choices, let us live in peace with one another. We do not want to be gullible women who believe whatever we hear and blindly do whatever we are told, nor do we want to give a place of prominence to old wives' tales. We want to be women of integrity and humility, exercising wisdom, and characterized by kindness, giving way to those who disagree with us.

CHAPTER FIVE

Loving the Kids:
Dinnertime, Bedtime, Holidays

> The voice of rejoicing and salvation is in the tents of
> the righteous. (Ps. 118:15)

Isn't it kind of God to actually command us to the delightful
task of loving our children? Older women (Tit. 2:4) are to
admonish the younger women to "love their children." What
a pleasant admonition that is. Loving our children involves
many duties, including training and discipline, but here we
are going to consider some of our daily activities that can
create an atmosphere of love and rejoicing in our homes.

God supplies us with motherly love for our children.
Even non-Christians love their children. But God wants us
to love our children even when they are not being lovable,
and this requires grace from God. We should be praying
that God will give us a godly, self-sacrificing, rejoicing
love for our children, even when we think we have enough
already. Little children can never have too much love. They
were made to respond to love, and when their little tanks
are full, they are secure and happy. When their tanks are
low, lots of odd behavior can show up. Each day has many
opportunities to love our children, but let's look at how
we can make the most out of dinnertime, bedtime, and
holidays. As Psalm 118:15 says, our "tents" should be noisy
with rejoicing. Our homes should be characterized by
much joy, and it isn't a quiet joy—it's loud. The righteous
have much to celebrate, and we should be rejoicing in our

salvation every day. We have daily opportunities to love our children and to teach them how to rejoice with us.

Let's start with dinnertime. I've mentioned Psalm 128:2-4, but it is important in several contexts. It provides a vivid picture of what mealtime should be. "When you eat the labor of your hands, you shall be happy, and it shall be well with you. Your wife shall be like a fruitful vine in the very heart of your house, your children like olive plants all around your table. Behold, thus shall the man be blessed who fears the Lord." Several principles can be found here that relate to the dinner table.

First we have the principle of eating the labor of our hands. Dinnertime is an opportunity to enjoy the fruits of our labor. Husband has been working hard all day, Mother has been working hard all day, and dinnertime is the result of all the labor. With no work, there would be no food. Remember from Genesis that God cursed the man in his calling, so it takes hard work to get food on the table. This, incidentally, should inspire us mothers to make dinner a time for our husbands to see and enjoy the fruit of their hard work. Proverbs 31:14-15 says the virtuous woman is "like the merchant ships, she brings her food from afar. She also rises while it is yet night, and provides food for her household." Preparing meals requires much time and effort, but it is a *good work* that we do for our families when we plan our meals, grocery shop, and cook. The way the table looks should be an accurate reflection of how hard Dad is working.

Next, notice that the mealtime is a happy time. The wife is compared to a grape vine, and in the Scriptures, wine is seen as a source of joy and an accompaniment to celebration: "And wine that makes glad the heart of man, oil to make his face shine, and bread which strengthens man's heart" (Ps. 104:15). The wife is a source of joy, bringing God's blessings into the heart of the house. Those little olive shoots around the table are some of the blessings she has brought forth. Dinnertime ought to reflect our thanksgiving for our many blessings, so it should be a time of rejoicing. "Go eat your bread with joy, and drink your wine with a merry heart; For God has already accepted your works" (Eccl. 9:7). From this we should see that when we gather around the table together for the evening meal (or any meal really), it should be a time of merriment, laughter, and rejoicing. Though not every dinner can be a feast, we can still enjoy the family sitting down together to eat the fruit of our labor. Even if it is a simple meal, it can be served festively when time is put into the way it looks, not just the way it tastes. Tablecloths, napkins, flowers, or candles all say, "This is going to be a wonderful time."

Over the years when we have had college students into our home, some have remarked that their family rarely sat down together for dinner. Often each person fended for himself. I read of a family with a stack of menus by the phone for each family member to order out his own dinner. Then each would retreat to his room and his own TV. This is a sad statement about the fractured American family. But with Mom and Dad both working away from home at full-time jobs, it's the only way to survive. In contrast, the Christian family has a wonderful opportunity to cultivate a love for God and a love for one another around the dinner table. Glorious times around the dinner table don't just happen. Mom has to put a great deal into the daily preparations.

Consider this proverb about mealtime: "Better is a little with the fear of the Lord, than great treasure with trouble. Better is a dinner of herbs where love is, than a fatted calf with hatred" (Prov. 15:16-17). What we want around our dinner table is the *fear of the Lord* and *love*. The menu is not the most important thing. We need to prepare our hearts as well as prepare the meal. Loving the children all day long, disciplining and training them, prepares them for a happy time at the table. If they are criticized or ignored all day, they will not be in a proper frame of mind to rejoice around the table with the family. Dinnertime should be what the family looks forward to all day. My children saved up lots of questions for their father for dinnertime. They looked forward to sharing funny things about the day, or they laid out their troubles before the family for help and counsel. This time became sacred to all of us, and when Dad was late from work, they were very reluctant to start the meal without him.

Hospitality should be something all the children participate in, but it should not be so often that they feel robbed of their time. Dinner is where we can give them our undivided attention. When our children were older, sometimes our meals could last one or two hours, depending on the discussions that developed. My daughter says that she was motivated to hurry with her school work so she could have plenty of time around the table.

Some did not grow up with a picture of regular family dinners. But this handicap can be overcome. We all eat every evening, so we have an opportunity every day to make this happen. We will learn as we go, get better as we go, and get ideas from friends. We began what we call our "sabbath feast" on Saturday nights when our children were college-age and our daughter was married. Because Sundays are a working day for a pastor, Saturday works best for us. Though we cannot get together every Saturday night, we have begun the tradition of a festive meal with wine where the whole family, including our grandchildren, sits down together. We push up the high chair and we all enjoy being together. As time goes by, we hope we will need another high chair, or even another table. Though it would have been nice if we had started this years ago, I am thrilled that we can begin now. Even though our children may be busy with many things, they can usually get together for a couple of hours with us Saturday evenings. Each family can arrange one meal a week (at least) to celebrate together. The Lord's Day is a perfect occasion and it comes weekly.

"Better is a dry morsel with quietness, than a house full of feasting with strife" (Prov. 17:1). The Lord knows that we women can get distracted over preparing a nice meal, and we can sit down to a beautiful table with a bad attitude. This is *not* how it should be. Sometimes with the hours of preparations we bring unspoken expectations that can backfire. Rather macaroni and cheese with joy than a turkey dinner with tension and resentment.

Dinnertime should *not* be a cranky time. If we insist on perfect manners from our children, dinnertime can become the nightly opportunity for spankings. Though we want our children to learn table etiquette, we should teach it cheerfully and be unwilling to sacrifice joy and happiness for strictness. Perhaps training can take place at lunchtime with an eye toward practicing at dinner. Though manners are very important, we must take care to insist first on the fear of God and love. God is not honored if we use the correct silverware with no love. Teaching table manners can be delightful when it is done in the joy of the Lord with patience and kindness. If the children feel that dinner is an inevitable obstacle course to get through each night, it cannot and will not be a joyful time. One family teaches their children to wait for mother (or the hostess) to sit down before taking a bite of dessert. If one of the children takes a bite before the appropriate time, their dessert is passed around the table and everyone gets to take a bite of it. This is a creative (and fun-loving) way to teach table manners.

If dinner conversation consists of arguing and complaining, it certainly will not be an enjoyable or appealing gathering. Neither should it be a time for everyone to dump all their complaints on the rest of the family. Grumbling, whining, and arguing should not be allowed. Rather, dinner should be a time when everyone can relax, enjoy the meal, listen to one another, and laugh together. Otherwise, it is just one more chore to get through. Making the meal time very rigid and formatted is not the answer. Trying to accomplish this by rote will not work, for then the children will not look forward to it, and it will seem phony and self-righteous.

The family gathered around the table is not only a foreshadowing of the table fellowship we will have in heaven at the marriage supper of the Lamb, but it is also a way we teach our children to approach the Lord's table at communion. Our table fellowship, the communion we have with one another, ought to be sweet, a good picture of that fellowship which will be much sweeter. God has given the Church two things: the Bible and the sacraments. We need to teach our children what communion around the table looks like. If our children grow up with a healthy view of communion with the family, this will easily transfer to their understanding of the Lord's supper. We should be regularly confessing our sins to one another to maintain good fellowship, and we should always be reflecting on our Lord's presence and work. That is why a father's presence is central to family fellowship around the table. He should be visibly the head. However, if the father is often gone or if he is entirely absent, a mother can do all within her power to make dinnertime all it should be. We can be encouraged by Eunice and Lois's examples to Timothy and realize that a missing father figure is a handicap, but it is not an insurmountable one.

Central to our table fellowship should be a love for words and the Word. Reading around the dinner table is a great way to integrate the two. This can include Scripture or poetry or recitations from the children or chapters from books you are reading together. And of course, it may have to move to the living room or the porch.

Whether you read at the table, between dinner and bedtime, or whenever you read, your children ought to develop a love for books, reading, and God's Word. Christians are to be people of the Book and people who love good books. The family gathered together over dessert listening to Dad read is a lovely tradition. (And if Dad doesn't want to read, there is no reason why Mom can't read to the kids at appropriate times.) Reading at bedtime, reading at dinnertime, reading on the porch on a summer evening—reading ought to be part of a family's heritage. Experiencing books together ties us together, and we begin to love certain books as a family and remember them like we remember a special vacation. We have family favorites that we never tire of hearing again. Mothers can work to provide time for the kids and Dad to read. This, like everything else, takes preparation. Finding good books and getting into the habit of reading is well worth the effort. Sometimes reading time could go for hours at our house. But families are dynamic. As babies come and children grow up, schedules will change. Older children can read to the younger ones, or reading may have to take place in shifts. The lovely thing about a family is that the relationships grow and deepen as the years go by. And though dinner may look a lot different when the kids are teenagers than when they were in booster chairs, the tradition is established. In the same way, when all the children are gone and you and your husband are home alone, dinner can still be a time of rejoicing though it may be much quieter. Then it's time for grandkids.

Like mealtime, bedtime happens every day and should be used as an opportunity for rejoicing together as a family. Singing and reading ought to characterize every evening. Psalm 149:5: "Let the saints be joyful in glory; let them sing aloud on their beds." Stories and prayers, hugs and back rubs should all make bedtime another blessed time together. It can conclude with father's benediction, a blessing spoken over each child, a prayer for the Lord's safekeeping for the night. Bedtime ought to be a fit conclusion to the evening spent in table fellowship, singing, and reading. Proverbs 3:24: "When you lie down, you will not be afraid; Yes, you will lie down and your sleep will be sweet." We ought to pray each night that our children will have sweet sleep. "He gives His beloved sleep" (Ps. 127:2).

Our children's beds should be happy places. They should be appealing, smelling fresh and clean, and feeling warm and snugly. Fluffy blankets, billowy pillows, warm comforters, and a favorite stuffed animal can make a big difference. They should enjoy their beds, and mothers can do much to keep the beds in good shape.

Bedtime can be a great opportunity to listen to our children. Just like everything else in a family, bedtimes alter as the children grow. Sometimes you will have opportunities with one child. You may have to rotate if you have a large family. Sometimes my children wanted me to lie down with them and make up stories together. These are happy, happy memories now. We must make the most of our opportunities and develop an atmosphere of love and fun. My father used to bring us treats at bedtime and make us guess fingers for them. This made bedtime a happy time when I was little. But my dad has always been a master of figuring out how to make *anything* fun.

When our children were very small (and our apartment not much bigger), all three of them slept in one bedroom: two in the bunk beds and one in the crib. Bedtime was quite a party. My husband Doug would bring in his guitar on hot summer evenings, and we would sing all manner of songs. The kids would request their favorites: "Summertime and the livin' is easy" or "Oh, little Rachel, oh," as well as the first hymn they ever learned, "Holy, Holy, Holy." After songs and prayers and kisses and drinks, the lights went out, but sometimes is was hard for little ones to believe all the fun was really over.

Occasionally after the bedtime ritual was over, Doug and I would stand by the front door and holler, "Jammy ride!" These magic words brought three bright-eyed children tumbling out of bed as if it was Christmas morning. Then into the back seat of the car they would scramble, amidst bathrobes and blankets (if it was chilly), and off we would go for ice cream cones.

Finally, another way we love our children is celebrating holidays together as a family. It is important that we teach them that God gives us special days of feasting together to celebrate His goodness and kindness to us. We ought not be afraid of what the pagans do. We can make the holidays anything we want them to be. Our children never missed Santa Claus because their Christmas wasn't about Santa. It was about rejoicing in the Incarnation of our Lord. Of course it involved lights, a tree, ornaments, stockings, gifts, candy, and a big party, but it was centered around Christ. Easter was not about the Easter Bunny, because it was a celebration of the Lord's resurrection. We did have a wonderful time coloring and hiding eggs because it was so much fun. We didn't worry that the pagans were doing it too. They weren't able to celebrate the resurrection in their Easters like we did. Some families may not need to color eggs because they have thought of something better. Of course that's okay too. We celebrated birthdays with money in the cake (an old family tradition), and the kids could always stay up as late as they wanted on their birthdays. Now as we hear our grown children reminisce about these things from their own perspectives, we realize how all the small joys added up to childhoods filled with happiness and hilarity that has carried over into their adult years.

It's never too late to start these things. Some families are way ahead of us in this area. We can learn from one another and grow some great family traditions. When I use personal examples, it is not because I think each family should read the books we read or celebrate together the way we do. Each family should develop its own culture and traditions together. Thankfully, no one pattern exists. Each family created by God will have a unique culture all its own, packed with its own customs, inside jokes, and memories. This is what it means to be a family.

We want our "tents" to be full of rejoicing. Laughter and jollity should be features of the reformed home. If God continues to be kind to us, we will all need to build bigger dining rooms and buy bigger tables for our feasting. We should cultivate celebration and gratitude in the fear of the Lord and with love, and what better way than around our tables with our children and grandchildren.

CHAPTER SIX

Manners:
Church Behavior, Friends, Family

> Finally all of you be of one mind, having compassion
> for one another; love as brothers, be tenderhearted, be
> courteous; not returning evil for evil or reviling for
> reviling, but on the contrary blessing, knowing that
> you were called to this, that you may inherit a blessing.
> (1 Pet. 3:8-9)

As we turn to the subject of manners and courtesy, this verse
has much to offer us. Notice that we are *all* to be of one
mind. We are to be compassionate toward one another. This
includes sharing in one another's sorrows and being urgent
to help. We are to love one another like brothers. We are a
covenant community; we are family. Our love should be a
family love. We are to be tender toward one another: tender
to protect each other's names and reputations, tender and
sympathetic to the needs of our brothers. The King James
renders *tenderhearted* as *pitiful*, full of pity. We are to be
courteous. This means we are to be gracious, considerate, and
kind. *Gracious* means full of grace. This sort of graciousness
cannot be self-generated. It is the result of God's kindness
and grace to us. We are to be a source of blessing to our fellow
Christians because *we were called to this*. And as a result of
our godly behavior, we will inherit a blessing. This is basic
Christian behavior. It is antithetical to a divisive, back-biting,
self-centered, and ill-mannered conduct.

   This is the Christ-centered mindset from which all good
manners should flow. As someone has said, good manners

are simply demonstrating love in trifles. This includes showing respect, putting people at ease, not monopolizing or manipulating but serving one another in love. It is putting our Christianity in practice and applying the golden rule. And of course, good manners should begin at home in the way we treat our husbands and children. We teach our children how to respect their father by showing them what it looks like. Wives should not treat their husbands like one of the kids but defer and honor them, submitting to and respecting them in the Lord. In other words, we must model Christian courtesy to our children, not simply expect it of them without showing them what it looks like.

Let's begin with church etiquette. Church manners have two aspects: worship and fellowship. 1 Corinthians 14:40 says in describing worship, "Let all things be done decently and in order." And in Colossians 2:5 Paul says, "Though I am absent in the flesh, yet I am with you in spirit, rejoicing to see your good order and the steadfastness of your faith in Christ." Our children are to worship with us, and they need to be taught that they must worship in a decent and orderly fashion. They must be trained and taught all week in preparation for worship. We cannot expect them to know how to behave without our instruction. The goal for our children is not that they sit still. That is simply the means to the end. The end or goal is that they worship God with us. Now little ones must be taught to sit still, but again, this is training to equip them for worship. Many families with little ones sit in the back so they will not be a distraction to others while they are training their children to sit quietly. Some families are way ahead of others, but as long as we are moving in the right direction, we should be pleased.

Methods of training vary, but the principle we should agree on is that our children should be expected to join in the worship of God at a very young age. We can share examples and ideas, but again, each family will vary in its progress. We must be compassionate and tenderhearted toward one another in this. One father loads his little toddler up with Cheerios outside before coming into worship, so hunger won't be a distraction. Some have their children practice sitting still during the week at home. Another father makes a list of words the children can read that will be in the sermon (like *law* or *love*) and has them make a tick mark on a sheet of paper each time they hear it. Now if some allow their children to color during the sermon, this should be seen as a temporary measure as they are training them to sit and listen. In other words, though we did not allow our children to do this, I do not want to be hard on those parents who are allowing it while they are getting their children up to speed. Some of the families in our church have come from backgrounds where the children have not had to sit through an hour-long sermon. So perhaps they can allow the children to color after they have listened for fifteen minutes and then stretch to twenty minutes the next week. This is an area in which we should bear with one another. On the other hand, if parents are allowing their children to play and color on the floor without training them to worship, they need to expect more of their children. Young children can be taught to "hold it" so they will not need to get up to go to the bathroom during church. By keeping liquids to a minimum and taking them to the bathroom before church, trips to the bathroom can be avoided. And with older children, it is not expecting too much of them to make them wait until the service is over.

As in all manners, the object is to serve others. Children who are whispering, shuffling papers, eating cookies and candy, or getting up to go to the bathroom are a distraction to others during worship. Mothers should work hard to prepare their children for the worship of God. This includes feeding them a good breakfast, taking them to the bathroom before church begins, as well as preparing them spiritually all week. Of course all parents rejoice when babies fall asleep during the sermon. But older children should be exhorted to pay attention and not be allowed to snooze. Families should worship together and not be scattered around the congregation with friends. This also allows the parents to see how the children are behaving during the service. Some churches have a section where all the teenagers are sitting with their friends. This should not be the norm for the church. Those college students away from home are in a different category, but they should be invited to sit with families whenever possible.

Other good manners during church would include participating in all the singing, following along during the Scripture reading, not looking around at others, not scratching or picking or chewing gum, and so forth. If the worship of God is the high point of our week, we should behave in an appropriate manner. Our children should wear their best clothes and be clean and tidy. They should be taught that our clothing affects our behavior and affects how other people will respond to us. If our children go to church in play clothes, no wonder they want to tear around and fidget.

When the saints gather together to worship, we will all be at different stages of our sanctification, so we ought not pride ourselves on our well-behaved children, nor should we look down on others who are still working on church manners. This is not courtesy.

During the fellowship time before and after church, much should be required of children. They need to be taught how to talk with adults. They should look them in the eye and speak. Shyness can really be rudeness. A child should not be allowed to hide his face (unless he is just a baby still) in mother's skirt when he's spoken to. This is a rudeness. A child must be taught to be respectful to older people, not cutting in front of them, but waiting till they pass through the doorway first. They must be taught not to run at church, and parents should always know exactly where their children are and what they are doing. My children had to stand with me after church while we visited, and I tried to include them in the visiting. If they wanted to go visit someone else, they simply had to ask permission, and they were not allowed to leave the room unless they checked with me first. This way

I did not have to go looking for my children when it was time to go. Children should not be allowed to interrupt, but neither should parents ignore their children when it is plain they want to speak to them. A little signal can be worked out, like a tap on the elbow if a child needs to speak to his mother. Then the mother can excuse herself for a moment to see to her child's needs. Children should also not be allowed to whine or moan or complain about how hungry they are and "can we go now?" Parents should keep their visiting to a reasonable limit so the children are not imposed upon, but children need to be taught that whining is not permissible anytime, especially not at church.

Now let's turn to the subject of friends. As we cultivate our own family culture of celebrating and rejoicing together, we are equipped and prepared to share with others in hospitality. Children can be taught to participate by greeting the guests, taking coats, helping with the preparations, sharing toys, and so forth. Learning to be a good host helps in learning how to be a good guest. When they go to someone else's home as a guest, you can prepare them by teaching them good manners. You can start with the simple things like teaching them to say *thank you* and *please* and picking up the toys before they leave. Children need to be taught to obey the house rules when not at their own home. For example, if the home they are visiting has a quiet rule, then your child should graciously comply, even if you don't have any such rule at your house. On the other hand, if your child knows you would not approve of his watching a video, he should be instructed on how to respond if his friend suggests a video. And a good guest always tells the hostess if he breaks or spills something. Your child should always tell you as well, so you can attempt to make restitution if need be. A good mother will always ask if her child was well-behaved while she was away. And of course, we ought not report petty things, but we should be careful to answer a parent truthfully about a child's behavior.

Sometimes mothers realize they need to teach on something that has never come up before. When my daughter was around four years old, I went to pick her up at a friend's house, and when she saw me, she moaned about going home. I had never thought about teaching my children how to greet me when I picked them up. But after that day my daughter always dropped what she was doing and ran to greet me with a big smile and "Hi, Mom!"

Sometimes house rules can be awkward, and here is where we especially must have love, meekness, and compassion. Consider the ways families differ in how they celebrate the Lord's Day. Some have rules about basketball or video games. If you are visiting another family, your child may not know about their house rules, and he may naively suggest a game that would put someone else in a tight spot. We ought to be able to stay out of any wrangles about how we honor the Lord on His day and relax about how others do it. If your child is unsure about something, he should feel free to ask you what you want him to do. Then you can be the bad guy when he tells his friend, "My parents don't want me to do that."

Finally, we must not short-change our own families when it comes to courtesy. We help our children present themselves to the world when we keep them clean and well-groomed. This is a courtesy to our children, and it is a courtesy to others. It is much more enjoyable to talk to a child who has a clean, shiny face, than a child with a dirty nose. This is simply the way we are made. We are honoring them when we wash their faces. Mothers should dress their children appropriately and teach them that dressing improperly can be discourteous. Hair hanging in their faces or sloppy, unkempt clothing is difficult to get past. Teaching them how to shake hands with clean hands, how to cough and sneeze discreetly, how to blow their noses quietly are all ways of loving them and loving all the saints. After all, manners are for others' sakes, not for our own sake. Just as teaching your child to chew with his mouth closed is for the benefit of everyone else at the table, in the same way, keeping your children tidy is for others.

If manners are not glorifying to God, then we ought not waste our time on them. But courtesy is a Christian characteristic; it is a means of serving God with gladness and rejoicing with all the saints in an orderly way.

CHAPTER SEVEN

Respecting Sons

> Beloved, I pray that you may prosper in all things and
> be in health, just as your soul prospers. (3 Jn. 2)

Bringing up children is a delightful privilege and an over-whelming responsibility. It is a high calling indeed. The phrase "bringing up" implies the goal of maturity. We are not to leave them as they are; we are to *bring them up* to their full stature both physically and spiritually. While we are to do all we can to present our children to God as faithful, fruitful servants, we must constantly lean on God, realizing it is all by His grace. God enables us, strengthens us, and provides us with wisdom, endurance, and love for our children. Apart from Him, our children cannot be "fat-souled," though we may read books on childrearing and plug Christian "formulas" for success. Notice the verse quoted above. Our souls should be prospering, and the apostle John is praying here that the saints' outward condition will be as prosperous as their inward condition. Parents should constantly consider what is good for their own souls and their children's souls. Modern Americans seldom even think about their souls at all. Christian parents must treat their children in such a way that their souls will prosper.

As we raise our children before the Lord with "rejoicing in our tents," it is helpful to make distinctions between our sons and daughters. Our culture wants to eradicate all differences and tell us that boys and girls are essentially alike apart from what we do to "program" them. This is foolishness. Sons and daughters are fearfully and wonderfully made, and we should not only acknowledge the distinctions between them, we should thank God and rejoice in these very marked differences. Christians should be clear thinkers when it comes to disentangling themselves from the egalitarian propaganda that pervades so much modern thinking. Especially when it comes to the important task of bringing up our children, we do not want to buy into the world's silly ideas about boys and girls.

Years ago I had taken my youngest in to see our pediatrician. My doctor was not available, so we visited one of his partners, a woman. While we were waiting to see her, my daughter and I were laughing over children's drawings that were decorating a calendar. When the doctor came in, we were still commenting on the funny differences between the boys' drawings (action pictures of airplanes, etc.) and the girls' pictures of flower-lined houses with smoke coming out of the chimneys. This distressed the feministic doctor who told us that the parents had obviously programmed the children to do this. We chuckled at her comments without engaging in a debate with her. But when we got to the car, my young daughter said, "She needs to have some kids." Even a small child can see the obvious.

As we strive to embrace truth, goodness, and beauty in our homes, we must be eager to love all that God has done in designing our children for their future callings as men and women. He has put it in the hearts of little boys to want to grow up to be doctors and lawyers, builders and preachers, firemen and farmers. Likewise, He has put it in the hearts of our daughters to want to be mommies. This is God's grace to us. These differences are design features that cannot be ignored. When we teach our boys that they will someday be providers and our girls that they will be homemakers, we are teaching with the grain, not against it. When government schools teach children contrary to God's purpose, they are messing with what God has ordained and will have to give an account to God for their disobedience.

Though most Christians would agree with this so far, sometimes we do not treat our children as though we believe it, and we end up being counterproductive in preparing them for their future callings. In this chapter we will consider how we should treat and train our sons and discuss what mothers can do to bring them up prepared to embrace their callings.

First let's address a son's need for respect. Wives are commanded in Scripture to respect their husbands (Eph. 5:33), and women are generally pretty poor at giving respect. This is why we need to be taught how. Our strength lies more in loving than in respecting. Just as men need respect from their wives, so sons need respect from their mothers and sisters. Of course, respect to your son will look different than respect to your husband, because your son is not in authority over you, but it is respect nonetheless. A woman's first priority must be to respect her husband. This is actually a significant way to respect sons. A woman should never drive a wedge between her sons and her husband by taking sides. She must render respect to her husband even when she disagrees with the way he is handling his sons. Certainly she should and must bring her concerns to him privately, but she should never tell her sons she disagrees with Dad unless it is clearly a moral issue. For example, if Dad is an unbeliever and wants the boys to shoplift or smoke pot, Mom must let them know that this is unacceptable. Abigail intervened when her husband was foolish. But this is not the norm. Rather, mothers often take sides with the son (and this is a form of mollycoddling), and he knows he can play her off Dad to get what he wants. This is destructive, disrespectful, unsubmissive behavior that requires repentance and restitution. Mothers, remember that Dad is the head. You must not take your duties of obedience lightly. Your son will respect you when you respect Dad. And sons should hear often from Mom's lips what a great Dad they have. This is important in growing healthy sons. Mothers must also learn how to respect their sons, and they must teach their daughters to respect their brothers. This not only prepares daughters to be practiced in giving respect, but it also teaches sons what they want to look for in a wife. What does this respect look like?

Respect to sons can begin when they are very young. As we go through this, please remember that Christian behavior will include respect for daughters and love for sons, but the emphasis here will be respect for sons and love for daughters. This is true in marriage as well, for husbands are to love their wives, but this does not mean wives don't need to love their husbands. Of course the converse is true as well: men must respect and honor their wives, but the Scripture's emphasis for them is love. As we discuss principles related to how we treat our children, it is certainly true that the Christian standards of behavior apply whether we are dealing with our sons or our daughters. The point here is to address what our primary focus should be.

When a mother respects her son, she verbalizes it. She praises him for his achievements. She expresses her admiration to him for his accomplishments. She gives him responsibility and expects him to fulfill his obligations. Respect is not the same thing as self-esteem. Modern self-esteem is not related to real performance. In fact, it's not related to anything. Respect is connected to real achievements. For little boys those achievements can be as simple as learning to tie their shoes, helping watch baby sister, or opening a door for Mom. Or it may be learning to read, "acing" a spelling test, memorizing Scripture, or kicking in a goal in a soccer game. It is important that respect is related to accomplishments, not just nebulous character traits. Respect should sound like this: "Son, I am very proud of you for teaching your sister to ride her bike. Thank you for being so patient with her." Or, it could sound like this when he's older: "I respect you for studying so hard and doing so well on your chemistry test. I am very proud of you." Words like *respect* or *admire* or *proud of* should be included in your expressions of respect to your sons.

Mothers should have high standards for their sons. If they fail in a job, mothers have to find something else to praise, but they must not lower the standard just to see their sons succeed. Boys who are braggarts or display bravado or exhibit other forms of misbehavior may be lacking in respect. Bragging is a form of showing off or looking for respect. If a young man's tank is full because of respect in the home, he will not have to do stupid things in front of his friends in an attempt to win their respect. A boy who is respected will have more confidence and be more prone to good behavior. "A wise son makes a glad father" (Prov. 10:1). Respecting a son can make him wise because he connects his good behavior with his parents' respect and honor for him. His parents' respect is important to him, and he will want to live in a manner that is consistent with their attitude and regard for him.

Another central aspect to respect is simple courtesy. A mother who is courteous to her children is respectful of them. A mother who makes fun of her son (or daughter) in public or tells others of his weaknesses or failures in casual conversation is showing disregard and disrespect. Pointing out our children's flaws is unkind. Making them feel foolish in front of others will breed resentment. We can take up their problems with them privately. There is no need to display them to the world. This is only humiliating and is certainly not modeling Christian behavior to our children. This courtesy is simply the golden rule again, treating our sons the way we want to be treated. When a mother shares things about her son, whether he is small or grown, that would embarrass him, she is tearing down her house. Telling people about his interest in a girl before it is public knowledge, laughing about his big ears, sharing about his concern over his acne—these are all examples of discourtesy and disrespect to sons.

On the other hand, telling your friends that your son made the dean's list or caught the pass for the winning touchdown is a way of publicly praising or respecting your son. Your friends should know this much: you are very, very proud of your sons. Their achievements should be a source of delight and joy to you, and that is something you should feel free to share with your friends. If they did not make the honor roll or win the science fair, you can still find something to praise them for but remember to link it to achievements and accomplishments.

We must prepare our sons to go out into the world, face obstacles, work hard, and provide for a household with integrity. Mothers can unwittingly undermine this preparation by mollycoddling their sons. If mothers are protecting and pampering their sons, they will grow up to be milksops (otherwise known as sissies), and obviously, this is not honoring to God. Our aim for our sons is maturity. We want them to be able to stand with their father against his enemies in the city gate (Ps. 127). We want them to be tough, not fragile. Mothers cannot fight their sons' battles, and they should not shelter them from consequences of their actions. For example, if a young man fails a test, Mom should not go to the teacher and ask for mercy. If the son has a good reason for failing (he was in the hospital with an appendicitis when they covered the material), then the son should go to the teacher and ask for an opportunity to make up the test. But if the failure was due to his own laziness, he should not be allowed to petition for grace. If a son lost a lawn-mowing job because he was constantly late or did poor work, parents should rejoice that God provides consequences to behavior in this world of His. Mother should not rush to a son's defense. However, her respect for her son should be shown in other areas where he is acting in an honorable way. I am convinced that a son who is respected and loved faithfully will be a respectable son and not the foolish son who is a grief to his father and mother (Prov. 10:1; 17:25). Sons who grow up looking to Mom to fix everything and go ahead of him smoothing out the road will look for the same thing in a wife: another mother to take care of him. Mothers must be hard-headed when it comes to sons and not rush in to protect them from the hard consequences of the world.

Sons must learn to take responsibility. This means they cannot be allowed to make excuses. Mothers must not indulge the tendency of sons to explain away their mistakes. Taking responsibility means not making excuses even when there is a good one. Mothers must not "feel sorry" for their sons when they fail. They must respect them through the failure, and one of the ways of doing this is by not encouraging excuse-making.

Mothers should also show respect by not being drawn into an adversarial relationship with their sons. The mother is in authority over her son (until he is grown) and should not argue with him as though she is arguing with an equal. Boys are very good at argumentation (my husband calls them sea lawyers), and they often can present many persuasive points for their case. And though mothers should be good listeners, they should refuse to be drawn into an argument. It would be better to take it up with Father later. Battles should be picked very carefully because it is essential that Mother win every time. And it is important that mothers not take things personally—getting hurt feelings and attributing motives. This will make the relationship a tangled mess, which is obviously not God-honoring. Mothers want to cultivate a good relationship with all their children. If Mom tells her son to please clean his room and he gives her fifteen reasons why that is impossible, she should not react by responding to his points with a counter argument. She should simply repeat her request with the added "and no backchat." Of course, Mom should be reasonable. If she is convinced by his reasons that this is not a good time, she can certainly say, "Fine. But it must be done before dinner. No clean room, no dinner." That's reasonable.

Boys can be ministered to in physical ways. They need food, they need sleep, and there really is no one like Mom when it comes to comfort. When small boys are hurt, Mother should look to their needs but not allow them to come unglued. "Shake it off! That's enough crying now." "Show me how to be tough." Don't tolerate a cry baby. Although it is understandable to see tears in young boys, older boys should not normally cry from pain. This may be an attention-getting device. Don't overdo on the comfort. If a son is grumpy, he may just be hungry. Make him a sandwich. Or he may need time alone. When my son was very young, I would sometimes pop him in the tub with a bunch of toys and a bowl of Cheerios floating. He would come out a changed man. My husband once asked me, "How did you know to do that?" I suppose it is mother's intuition. But boys should not be waited on hand and foot. They should be participating in the work in the home, but they should not be tied to it like the girls are. Let me explain.

Boys should *not* be trained to be home-centered. Even if they are homeschooled, they should be taught that the pattern of the home is not the pattern of their future life. They are to grow up prepared to go out into the world to conquer it. If they are domesticated, they will be unfit to do battle with the world on any level. Boys need the rough and tumble of getting their heads knocked once in a while, and Mom cannot be there to pick up the pieces every time. This may sound harsh, but boys need to bump up against the realities of life. Otherwise they will not be able to stand their ground when they come into conflict in the world. If they spend all their days in Mom's environment, they will not have a good picture of what it means to be a man. This is a very real threat to the church; we need strong, godly men to be leaders in their homes and in the church. Mom cannot be the role-model for her sons. Though she is the center of his world when he is a baby, a son must shift over to seeing his father as his role-model. This is very, very important. He must be taught to love, admire, and appreciate his mother, but he must learn very early on that he must follow in his father's footsteps, not his mother's. Mollycoddling is a common problem. That's why we have terms in our language like *sissy, tied to the apron-strings*, etc. Boys like to be coddled and mothers like to coddle, but this has devastating and long-term consequences.

Self-control is what we want to teach our sons, for this is what they will need in the world. A little boy who is indulged and allowed to cry and sob and stomp when he doesn't get his way will someday be throwing tantrums on the basketball court. This is when a son becomes a public embarrassment. You want your son to be self-governed, so he will not have to be governed by someone else; in this case, it might be by the coach or ref who rightly throws him out of the game or off the team. This sort of self-discipline will be very necessary when your son is old enough to begin looking for a wife. Many an undisciplined young man has gotten a girl pregnant. When he reaches this age, he is old enough to not only ruin his own life, but other lives as well. Boys will not suddenly acquire self-discipline when they are eighteen and in real danger of messing things up. Mothers must begin to train them to be self-controlled before they are two years old. I have seen my daughter do this with her little boy (who, as I write this, is not yet two). When he bonks himself and starts to cry, she gives him a hug and then says, "Show me tough." The amazing thing is, he does. He stops crying and he shows her what tough is. This is not a form of repression or oppression; this is training up a young man in the way he should go, and it gives me no end of joy to see my grandson growing up to be a man.

Finally, regarding sons, we must not expect male piety to look like female piety. Boys may not be inclined to write their favorite verses for Mom and post them on the fridge or put them beside her bed. Though his sisters may express their love for God this way, a young man may express his godliness by telling the neighbor boy to shut up when he takes the Lord's name in vain in the back yard. Mothers must be careful to make proper distinctions. If sons are seeing the antithesis between the world and godly living, mothers should be pleased and delighted. Because women naturally exhibit their piety in feminine ways, we can be quick to misjudge male expressions of the same piety. Be cautious not to assume your son is doing poorly because he is not sharing more about his personal Bible reading and so forth. Look for the way he engages with life and its follies. If a Christian boy shows up with bleached hair, a mother ought to rejoice when she hears that her son told him, "I see we've been thinking through our actions again." This sort of sarcastic reproval is a good sign of masculine thinking. Don't expect your son to be tender the way a daughter is. Unfortunately, today much of the church's teaching is centered around teaching men to think and act like women. This is foolishness, and we ought not participate in it.

Daughters are simple for mothers to understand because they know what women are like. But because of this, mothers can be too hard on the girls and too soft on the boys. Conversely, dads can be too hard on the boys and too soft on the girls. But God can give us all wisdom so we are thinking clearly and making good judgments. This will ensure that our children's souls are prospering under the blessing of God.

CHAPTER EIGHT

Loving Daughters

> And in all the land were no women found so fair as the daughters of Job: and their father gave them inheritance among their brethren. (Job 42:15)

If you are blessed in your home with both sons and daughters, you will have many opportunities to laugh about the differences between men and women. Brothers are good for sisters, and sisters are good for brothers. But if all your children are of the same sex, this is a different kind of blessing, but a blessing all the same. I am convinced there are no bad combinations; children are a blessing.

Mothers should be naturally very good at raising daughters because, after all, they are women like we are. But sometimes mothers can become exasperated with their daughters for that very reason: they are so much like us.

The first thing mothers must remember in raising young women is to be kind. A critical spirit is a destructive thing, and mothers must not be too hard on their girls. Mothers are naturally prone to be easier on the guys, but this must not be. Mothers must not attribute motives to their daughters, nor take offense, nor lose patience, nor take things personally as they are raising their daughters. Rather they should put on tender mercies. This is a tall order, but we must not cut ourselves slack when it comes to holiness. Women are the role models for their daughters, and they must teach them about meekness, submission, respect, deference, courtesy, and holiness by example. This does not mean that a mother of sons does not have to model these graces. But daughters must look to their mothers as primary examples of their future callings.

Daughters primarily need love and security. This is why a critical spirit is so destructive. Remember, we want our children to have fat, prospering souls. Criticism and impatience destroy rather than build up. Daughters need to feel important, loved, accepted, needed, wanted, and appreciated. Mothers must be diligent to praise their daughters, not for their achievements primarily, but for who they are. Though daughters are not normally built with the love of competition, like the boys are, they do feel a sense of competition with other women, including their sisters. Mothers must do all they can to nurture security and acceptance and never compare one sister to another. Each daughter will have special gifts and special needs. It is mother's job to help identify these gifts and encourage the exercise of them. It is also mother's job to identify special needs and do all she can to meet them. Mothers can be of real help to fathers in this area, for they can point out that Susie is needing some time with Dad.

Boundaries help establish a feeling of security for daughters. Though sons need boundaries for their own protection, daughters need them for security. They want to know that there is a rock-solid wall of protection around them, and even if they squawk about it from time to time, they hate it if the wall is squishy and gives in with a little push.

Little girls exhibit a low tank by looking for attention, usually by whining and complaining rather than by outright rebellious behavior. If they do not get attention, certainly their behavior can become rebellious. Daughters have a built-in, God-given need for male attention. This is why God in His Providence gave them fathers. Though Mom needs to pour on the love and attention, Dad must as well because this fulfills the need for male approval. Mothers can encourage (not nag) their husbands to love on their daughters and encourage daughters to love on Daddy. When a daughter is not getting enough attention from the God-appointed men in her life, she may become friendly to strange men. This should be a warning sign to you. If she climbs up on the laps of strangers in your home, you should be alarmed. Dad needs to start dishing out the hugs. In the case of a single parent, God can provide this male attention through a grandfather, uncle, or even an "adopted" grandfather. When daughters are little and looking for male attention, it can be an annoyance. But a teenage daughter will learn that she can get attention from men without being annoying anymore. Most promiscuity in women is not a desire for sex, but a desire for security and love. When daughters do not get sufficient male attention from Dad, they will look for it elsewhere when they are old enough. They need lots of love, hugs, understanding, and reassurance. Mothers are naturally good at giving love, but little girls are bottomless pits for love, so both Mom and especially Dad need to pour it on. If a father is unwilling to give his daughter love, a mother cannot force it. She can make things worse by complaining, arguing, and nagging at her husband. On the other hand, she can trust God to supply, and she can do all in her power to meet her daughter's needs.

Daughters need to be taught to control their emotions and should not be allowed to use them to manipulate to get their way. Mom must show the way here, as in other areas, by her example. Whining, gossiping, and complaining should not be allowed; rather thanksgiving, humility, and submission should be taught from the beginning. Little girls should be comforted when they are hurt, but at some point they should be told, "Okay, that's enough now." Emotions must be taught to follow and not allowed to lead. Mothers who successfully teach their daughters this will save them much heartache and misery in the years ahead. In adolescence when the hormones kick in, daughters must be taught that they may not use "hormones" as an excuse for sin, be it grumpiness or irritability. Tears are fine when they are not self-centered and resentful. Tears are never the problem, they are the symptom. If girls are allowed to indulge tears for whatever reason, they will not have mastery over their emotions. They should be taught that it is wrong to take offense as well as to give offense. Tears have a place, but they should be rare and brief. Even in the case of a real loss, such as the death of a loved one, there is a time to cry and a time to cease from crying. If we don't watch carefully, tears quickly turn into self-pity and anger. We must watch over our daughters and teach them to control themselves. If little girls can cry to get their way, they will keep acting childishly when they are grown.

This same principle applies to silliness. Little girls can be silly to a fault. Here again, mothers must exercise wisdom so they can say when enough is enough. Too much giggling and silliness leads to sins of indiscretion. Self-control on both fronts (tears or laughter) is needed.

Daughters, unlike sons, should be taught to be home-centered. If a daughter is attending a Christian day school that takes her out of the home, Mother needs to compensate by spending lots of time on the domestic arts. Quilting, cooking, cleaning, babysitting, decorating, and gardening are all activities that can keep a daughter from losing her home-centered focus. Again, Mom is the role model. If she is home-centered, it is likely her daughters will follow her lead. This should not be too difficult because when girls are home (even if they attend school), they will be naturally inclined to learn the domestic arts, and chances are that Mom needs enough help that she will ensure that her daughters learn one way or the other. Of course parents should teach their daughters that all of their education is to prepare them to be very smart wives and mothers. I am convinced that what the parents do and teach in the home will guide them to this, even if they are at school each day.

Sometimes a daughter is positively resistant to domesticity and wants to be a tomboy. Though a little of this can be cute, too much is a positive evil. Many parents are afraid to make decisions that they think their children will not like. That is a ridiculous notion. Parents are supposed to make decisions their children won't like—that's why we tell them to put on their seat belt or eat their peas or do their homework or go to bed. When a daughter is rejecting her femininity when she is little, it doesn't look too dangerous. But when she is older, the problem becomes more obvious. Though I am not suggesting that all little girls be forced to wear ribbons in their hair, I do think parents are obligated to see that their little girls are feminine and like it. This means combining the requirement of dresses or ribbons with teaching on how God made the world and why it is good. It is difficult for women in their twenties to overcome their lack of femininity because they feel awkward and unnatural in a dress or wearing lipstick. Mothers must make sure their daughters are comfortable with their femininity at an early age. We are born toward the direction of our sex, but it must be encouraged too. This means not allowing certain things (like baseball caps) and requiring certain things (like wearing dresses or rocking the baby) when they are little. And even if they resist at first, they will grow to embrace these things. Obviously, some girls must be held back because they are way too eager for pierced ears and high heels, but here I am speaking of those daughters who want to be tomboys.

At the same time, as mothers model and teach a biblical femininity, modesty and propriety should be central to the teaching. Just getting your daughter to love pretty dresses is certainly not the goal. We need to teach them that God created beauty and that it is good, but He also put bounds around it. We must not make the mistake of teaching them that the woman on the cover of *Cosmo* is yucky. If she were yucky, none of the men would be interested, and it would be a waste of time for the magazine to display her on the cover. No, she doesn't look yucky. The female body is beautiful. But modesty teaches us it is not for the world to enjoy; rather, it is for a husband to enjoy. This doesn't require us all to wear potato sacks. We should enjoy our femininity, work to be beautiful, and yet not go beyond what is decent and modest.

We emphasized to our daughters the importance of being beautiful on the inside first. Then we could rejoice in the beautiful dress because it was a good reflection of what was on the inside. We must teach our daughters the importance of this priority.

In some quarters of the Church today, women are taught that they should not wear makeup, get their hair colored or permed, and that they should look plain and not attract any attention. This is certainly not a biblical standard. We should not put our trust in our beauty, but we should use our beauty to delight our husbands as well as to enjoy ourselves and please our children. We should be moderate in all things, but we ought not to reject beauty helps if they are reasonable and helpful.

Our culture is far from home-centered; rather, it is bedroom-centered. We certainly do not want our daughters to be bedroom-centered. One way the world teaches little girls to be bedroom-centered is through the propagation of Barbie dolls. She is an oversexed twinkie with no brains. While baby dolls encourage little girls to pretend to be mothers, Barbie dolls encourage girls to pretend to be Barbie, to imitate her, and to want to grow up to be "just like Barbie." Ken only creates more opportunities for being bedroom-centered. Now some may say that their daughters play with Barbie in a pure way. But I would encourage you to think this over. If a girl plays with Barbie in a God-honoring way, it is going to get boring really fast. Barbie can't cook dinner very well in her evening gown and spiked heels. Even if the play itself is "pure," it can lead to covetousness and worldliness. Look closely at Barbie, her clothes, her accessories. Are these good for your daughter's soul? Most of her clothes look like the garb of a hooker. Her body is the world's lustful ideal: big breasts, long skinny legs, etc. Toys are teaching our children just like the books they read are teaching them, and Christian parents must think biblically about every aspect of life. Consider whether Barbie is the kind of role model you want for your daughters. Baby dolls can be rocked, changed, fed, burped, just like Mother does with the real baby. This encourages a home-centered, family-centered paradigm. But Barbie and dolls like her encourage our daughters to have the world's ideas about modesty, propriety, and decency.

Even though daughters may like to push the limits, as I said before, they love boundaries that are immovable. This gives them tremendous security and provides an environment in which they can flourish. If they are allowed to manipulate to push the boundaries, they will truly be unhappy in the long run, even if they like the short-term benefits of getting their way. Daughters should grow up understanding that they are to be protected primarily by Dad, but also by Mom. Even brothers can play a role in this protection. Daughters have to be taught to say "no" to guys on the street (or on the phone) who ask them out. They need to have a healthy dose of realistic teaching on the nature of men and a comparable dose of "rudeness" teaching. Many girls are too polite to guys, so they end up tolerating a lot of foolishness. We must teach our daughters how to communicate firmly as a means of protecting them. And we must not be afraid to say "no" to our daughters either.

Finally, just as sons need to be taught to be kind to their sisters, daughters must be taught to respect their brothers. This means not teasing them in ways that would embarrass them, or sharing stories with girlfriends about what dumb thing their brother did. Daughters should have a high regard for their brothers and should be taught by Mom how to communicate it.

As we apply these principles of loving and respecting our children, they will grow up in an environment where they have seen what God's pattern for marriage should be. And this pattern in the home is the best preparation they can have for their own marriages. Not only will they have a picture of respect and love, they will have practiced these things themselves. These are the kind of prosperous children who will rise up and call their parents and families blessed.

CHAPTER NINE

Setting Standards:
God's Rules and House Rules

> Be diligent to know the state of your flocks, and
> attend to your herds. (Prov. 27:23)

This is a wonderful verse when you think of applying it to
your own little flock of children. We are called to be wives
and mothers. Next to respecting and honoring our husbands,
caring for our children is our primary duty before God.
Notice in this verse, we are to be *diligent* to know how our
children are doing. This takes time. How is each one of your
children doing spiritually, emotionally? It is your responsibility to find out. We must *attend* to our children, or to put
it another way, we must give them our *attention*.

Sometimes Christian women become unhappy about
the "state of their flocks," and they feel like failures when
it comes to their children or their homemaking abilities. So
they look around for another "ministry" they can be involved
in where they can feel successful. "They made me the keeper
of the vineyards, But my own vineyard I have not kept"
(Song 1:6b). We must keep our own vineyards before we
expand to take on more responsibility. God has given us our
children as our "ministry." We must not look elsewhere for
fulfillment or success. We must excel where He has put us,
and after we have a thriving, healthy vineyard, we certainly
may look around for more ground to work. But be careful
not to become involved in Christian work outside the home
unless your herds are attended to, your vineyard is kept, and
you still have time to give. First things first.

Our children are our *disciples*. Not only must we be diligent to know how they are doing, we must be godly examples so that they can imitate the behavior we model to them. We must not expect any Christian behavior from our children that we have not laid out before them in our own lives. Do not expect your children to be kind unless they see you being kind. Do not expect them to be cheerful if you are always grumbling. You are the discipler of your children. You not only teach, you give constant, close-up examples and applications of your teaching every day. We must pay close attention to our children. And of course, there will be many opportunities for discipline. Discipline for the disciple is not optional.

If we love our children, as we must, we will discipline them: "He who spares the rod hates his son, but he who loves him disciplines him promptly" (Prov. 13:24). If you see a little nine-month-old baby showing his anger, it may be funny or cute. But if a parent loves that child, the parent will see that the anger is disciplined at its first appearance. If a parent hates the child, when you see that child a couple of years later, it will be frightening. A bad temper that is allowed to grow will become tyrannical behavior in the grocery store. You've seen those kids. Those children who throw fits in public are hated children. The parents have indulged them and have let sin have its ugly way. And undisciplined children are unloved children.

Christian parents don't just want to discipline their children. They want to discipline them in a godly way, a biblical, God-fearing, and God-glorifying way. This requires commitment and hard work, but the result is godly offspring (Mal. 2:15). Godly discipline must demonstrate two things: our obedience to God and our love for our children. When one of these is missing, we will either have ungodly discipline or no discipline at all. God has commanded that parents assume the responsibility of discipline, and He has commanded us to love our children. So Christian parents must assume that when they discipline properly, they are loving and obeying God, as well as loving their children. This should give us an earnestness and an eagerness to do it right. Methods for discipline will vary among parents, but the Scriptures do lay out certain principles that can guide us as we discipline our children.

Godly discipline should always be in the context of a warm, loving atmosphere, not in an environment of criticism and harshness. If you are constantly "on your children's case," this is not discipline. Rather it is you whining and complaining about your child to your child. God overlooks so much in us. If the Holy Spirit convicted us of every sin, every day, every time, we would be miserable people. But He is longsuffering toward us and delights to show mercy. He does not overwhelm us with correction and commands, but gently leads us and chastens us. This kind of discipline "yields the peaceable fruit of righteousness" (Heb. 12:11), but the mother who whips her child with her tongue day in and day out will yield a crop of bitterness and resentment and probably rebellion as well. We want our children to enjoy their family, their time at home, their time around the table. "But surely every little failure need not be censured," says Matthew Henry. If they are berated and accused and constantly corrected, their lives will be a grief to them, not a joy. They should receive lots of love, encouragement, and praise, not just correction.

Godly discipline is focused on the long-term goal of maturity, not a short-term desire to make life easier for ourselves now. God always desires maturity (Eph. 4:14-15). "Brethren, do not be children in understanding; however, in malice be babes, but in understanding be mature (1 Cor. 14:20). This does not mean that we despise our children's immaturity. It simply means that we are eager to see them pressing on to the next thing while we enjoy and delight in where they are now. We want our children to grow to be godly men and women. This takes years of love and discipline. We must always remember the goal and realize that each correction should take our children closer to this goal of maturity. If it doesn't, then it is probably not godly discipline.

Godly discipline is not for the parents' sake, but for the children's sake. If you are disciplining because you have "had enough of that," then you are not disciplining properly. Your discipline should not be the result of your impatience or anger. If you are angry, you are not fit to discipline your child; you need discipline yourself. If you allow bad behavior to go undisciplined until you lose your patience, you are not disciplining in a godly fashion. Your discipline should always be for your child's sake, to teach and conform him to the Word of God. It should not be because you want a little peace and quiet.

Godly discipline is biblical, not sentimental. We should want to be hard-headed (yet tender-hearted), clear-thinking, Bible-reading Christians who are not soft on sin either in ourselves or in our children. At the same time, we should be merciful and kind-hearted. We should not give way to pity and sentiment when correction is needed—"Oh, the poor little buddy." This is not going to result in godly offspring. There is a love that indulges and ultimately kills. But that is not a biblical love at all; it is a hatred of our children. Jesus said, "If you love me, keep my commandments" (Jn. 14:15). If we love God, we will obey Him. If we love our children, we will teach them to obey us, and when they are older, they will obey God as well. Obedience is central to the Christian life. When our children are old enough to understand God's commandments, they should know what obedience looks like because they have grown up being taught to be obedient children.

Godly discipline will provide tremendous security for our children. A child who knows where the boundaries are and that they are enforced is a secure child. This security will be in their parents, and when they are older, they will transfer this security to God. If their security is not in their parents, but in a blanket or a toy, they will be insecure. How can a child learn to transfer his confidence from a six-inch blanket remnant to God? It is much easier to trust God the Father if they have learned from an early age to trust their earthly father and mother.

When children are dinky, they must be disciplined for attitudes. Parents must discuss how and when discipline should begin, but usually somewhere between age one and two, most children will need some form of discipline. A wife's faithful discipline of her little disciples will be a means of honoring and respecting her husband as well as a means of obeying and glorifying God. "The heart of her husband safely trusts her" (Prov. 31:11). Her husband knows that she will not let ungodly behavior go without discipline while he is gone.

Discipline is not punishment. Punishment is meted out as a judicial payment for wrongdoing. Discipline brings repentance and correction. Discipline is training that produces self-control and builds character. Punishment is not meant to be corrective, so our children should not be punished, but disciplined. Discipline is for disciples.

In many ways, disciplining children is a means of disciplining parents, for it takes hard work and effort and perseverance to discipline faithfully before God. Remember that parents are responsible to God for how their families turn out. We must not compare or envy other households. As we apply biblical principles, we will have different approaches. We do not need to walk in lockstep; we must walk in Christ. We must seek to honor God with the children He has given us and not spend our time seeing how other people do it or don't do it. In other words, we must mind our own business. Consider some of the following principles as you discipline your children.

Listen to your children. Look them in the eye when you talk to them and when they are talking to you. Don't ignore them when you are talking with friends at church, at the grocery store, or on the phone. Sometimes bad behavior can be an attempt to get attention, and from their perspective, any attention is better than no attention. A low tank can result in whining, fighting, or just plain disobedience. Not only is discipline needed, but lots of love is needed to correct the problem.

Children need a picture of what repentance looks like, and they should see it in their parents. When parents sin, parents should ask for forgiveness, and if the children saw the sin, the children should see the repentance.

Be positive when you talk about your children, in or out of their hearing. Don't complain about your lack of time for yourself, or how hard it will be to have them all around over summer vacation. I always hated hearing about the terrible twos, and I wondered if they could be that bad. Finally, a friend told me that she called them the terrific twos, and I have thought of them that way ever since. Children in our culture are generally viewed as an imposition and a bother. Though I think even the pagans would say they love their kids, they don't talk to them or about them as though they really do. What a pleasure it was recently, while sitting in a doctor's office, to hear an older woman say, "I raised six children, and I would do it all again." What a delight to hear such a positive statement.

Mothers, because they are busy people, are quick to say "No." Sometimes we should stop and think about whether a "Yes" is possible. Maybe we should say, "Well, let me think about that." Or maybe we have another idea. Don't always say "No." Find some things you can say "Yes" to around your house. Have a "Yes" shelf in the living room or a "Yes" drawer in the kitchen for the toddlers, so everything in the house isn't a "No." Even if you don't feel like getting out the play dough, perhaps you really could. Often mothers say "No" just out of laziness. Children need to hear "Yes" and not just the automatic "No."

Be consistent. Decide what behavior is worth disciplining and stick to it. Make sure that the issues are not unimportant so that your child is not overloaded with commands. For example, if you tell your child in the grocery cart to say hello to Mrs. Smith, you must be prepared to discipline if your child does not comply. Be wise in what you command. Perhaps it would be better to prepare the child about saying hello at home and tell him that you will remind him when he forgets.

Discipline for attitudes when the children are little: defiance, grumpiness, anger, whining (to name a few). Be realistic about what you expect of your children, prepare and remind them. Remember that bad behavior can be the result of a low tank. Pour on the love, affection, encouragement, and comfort all the time. Be clear about what you expect.

You may have shopping rules, phone rules, bedtime rules, company rules, playing rules, dinner rules, and so forth. Don't overwhelm your children by expecting them to remember them all. Remind them in a cheerful way, not a threatening, negative tone. Lighten up. Some of my husband's bedtime rules for our children were "No playing with the moon!" and "No throwing snowballs!" and "No walking on the ceiling!" They loved his playfulness.

Discipline should be chastising, painful, and always followed by comfort and forgiveness. Though it should be painful, it should never damage the child. A swat on the bottom should not leave bruises, and of course, a child should never be slapped across the face or jerked around.

Discipline should happen at home, not at the grocery store or the neighbor's house. Remember we are not to provoke our children. We should not keep them up past their bedtime talking with our friends and then discipline our children for whining. Of course they should always be held to a high standard, but perhaps in that case, it is the parent who should be disciplined for irresponsibility and self-centeredness.

In teaching our children, of course God's rules should be emphasized over house rules. House rules are eventually lifted, but God's rules are never lifted. Eventually you should not need to tell your child to brush his teeth or hang up his towel. But God's rules about lying, stealing, sassing Mom, fighting or quarreling with sister, whining, or refusing to say hi to Grandma are always in effect. The teen years should be characterized by lifting house rules, not slapping on new rules. If godly discipline has been applied when the children are little, the parents will reap the fruit of self-governed, godly children. As the children get older, they should have more say about how their room is arranged or what they wear or what time they go to bed. Tastes differ, and children should have an opportunity to choose what they like in more and more areas.

In the teen years, if the parents have attended to their children properly, there will probably be little bumps but no major battles. If, on the other hand, the spade work has not been done, wise parents will need to pick their battles carefully. Parents ought not to be afraid to say "No" if necessary. Titus 2:11-12 tells us that we have to be taught by the grace of God to deny ungodliness and worldly lusts. Parents have to teach their children to say "No" to ungodliness. They must be taught, not just commanded. Innocence in our children is not preserved by ignorance. We want moral integrity in our children. We want them to grow up to be godly men and women who are obedient to God's Word. Just throwing away the TV may preserve their ignorance, but it does not teach them to think like a Christian or to be morally upright.

Parents should be teaching their children about the culture around them from the time they are tiny. They should understand why they are not attending the government schools. From the time they are old enough to know what marriage is, they should know that they will not marry a non-Christian. Principles of modesty and propriety in dress, principles of dating or courtship, and entertainment standards should all be taught and discussed from a very young age. Girls should grow up expecting that it is Dad's job to protect them from the boys. Boys should be guided in their understanding of covenantal protection. They should have a very high regard for the principle of a father's protection over his daughters and know that he has no business fooling around with girls until such time that he can offer covenantal protection himself.

Parents should not be too busy for their teenagers, even though they can take care of themselves. They need their parents' ears and eyes, and they still need much love, guidance, and understanding. Though they need independence and privacy, they should not be allowed to be sullen or introverted. Parents should be willing to drop what they are doing to listen to their kids. Our children need time, even when they are grown, and a wise parent will not put them off.

Sometimes parents put too much responsibility on their children's shoulders, expecting them to make decisions that the parents should be making for them. For example, children shouldn't be given the choice of homeschool or Christian school or public school. The average child is not mature enough to carry the weight of such a decision and will certainly not want to bear the responsibility of the consequences of such a decision. Wise parents won't allow children to guide such important decisions.

Standards of Christian behavior, or God's rules, are never lifted. But as our children reach maturity, we will want to give them more liberty to see that the standards we have taught them have really been internalized. A responsible sixteen- or seventeen-year-old can be given the liberty to make decisions regarding what movies to watch, for instance. If a parent has taught the child properly, a wise child will not race off to watch all the movies he wasn't able to watch when he was under the parents' supervision. If the parents remove "house rules" and the child displays irresponsibility, it may have been too soon for the removal of the training wheels, and parents may need to resume control of that area. But our children should grow up knowing that we plan to lift control and allow them to make decisions for themselves. If we clamp down during the teenage years, we may provoke rebellion instead.

Mothers are in a unique position to know the state of their flocks. They must make the most of all their opportunities to love and guide and discipline and train their children, under their husband's authority and to the glory of God. Then we will be pleased, with Him, to see godly offspring.

CHAPTER TEN

The Importance of Education

> The fear of the Lord is the beginning of knowledge: but
> fools despise wisdom and instruction. (Prov. 1:7)

Scripture makes it very clear that *parents* are responsible for
the godly education of their children. "And you fathers, do
not provoke your children to wrath, but bring them up in
the training and admonition of the Lord" (Eph. 6:4). The
Greek word for *admonition* here is a word used to include
education or enculturation. This means fathers must pass
on all that the culture encompasses to their children. When
do they do this? "You shall teach them diligently to your
children, and shall talk of them when you sit in your house,
when you walk by the way, when you lie down, and when
you rise up" (Deut. 6:7).

Christians have the responsibility and opportunity to
educate their children in a God-honoring, God-glorifying
way. This means education is not optional. If you cannot
afford to educate your children, you cannot afford children.
It's that simple. Parents who think that education is unnecessary or superfluous do not understand God's commands
above. Education must begin with parents. Mothers have a
unique role in the education of their children. Since God
has called wives to be helpmeets for their husbands, a large
part of this help will come in assisting with the educational
process. But first we must value education and determine to
be life-long learners ourselves. Mothers must be learners and
readers themselves so they can model to their children the

joy and love of learning. We cannot expect our children to love learning if we don't. We want them to see their learning as a means to an end, not an end in itself. And of course, the end is bringing glory to God. As mothers, we glorify God as we learn more about His world and rejoice in all He teaches us about His creation. If we are grateful and eager learners, our children will be as well.

If we want our children to understand the Bible and understand the world in light of God's Word, we must teach them to be logocentric and bibliocentric. The Word is God's means of communicating His love to us. Christians, above all people, should be word lovers, book lovers, and especially lovers of God's Word. The study of the Scriptures cannot be seen as one more subject for our children to study while they also study math and literature. The Bible provides the light by which our children can study math and literature and science and language.

We want our sons to grow up to lead their families and to provide faithfully for them. We want our daughters to grow up to be exceptional helpmeets for godly husbands. This requires much preparation, education, and training. As we examine the importance of education, I want to look at some of the dangers, misconceptions, and temptations that will sidetrack parents or distract them away from their calling to educate their children.

One of the central dangers in this area is abdication on the part of parents. Whether parents choose to enroll their children in a Christian school, homeschool them, or use tutorials, oversight is required by the parents. It is possible to do well with all three options, but it is also possible to abdicate in all three. If you enroll them in a Christian school, you may be tempted to be uninvolved, assuming that the administration is holding the teachers accountable. Of course, a good Christian school will do this. But do you know your children's teachers? Do you know what they are teaching? Have you read the school's vision statement? Do you know their philosophy of education? A good parent will strive to be involved in these areas.

If you are homeschooling, the temptation is to assume that abdication is impossible. However, there are just as many ways to abdicate at home. You may send them off to the library to read, but what are they reading? Are they thinking about what they are reading? Or you may decide that you're too busy for school today. This is how different subjects can fall to the ground. Homeschooling requires constant oversight and accountability, just as a Christian day school does.

Finally, if you are using tutorials you must also exercise oversight. This is where a parent can fall between two stools. You think you are homeschooling because they are not enrolled in a day school, so you assume you are exercising oversight. But your children are sitting under tutors. Who are they? What is their world view? What kind of accountability do they have? What sort of materials are they using? Are these people Christians? All this requires diligent oversight because sin is everywhere.

As Christian parents study education itself, we must beware of unbiblical thinking surrounding the subject. One such example of unbiblical thinking is the issue of character versus knowledge. This mindset sounds something like this: "My children are not studying math and science right now because we are working on character." Or, "John is failing history, but we are so pleased with his character development." This is ridiculous, and it can show up in both homeschool and day school students and parents. It is not as though Christian parents must choose between academics and character. That is an absurdly false dilemma. Much character is built in students as they work on academics. This is really just a flimsy excuse for laziness. If Christians really had to choose between character and academics, it would be easy. We would all agree that character is more important. It sounds very pious to be focusing on character, but it can simply be an excuse for not working hard on science and math. Proverbs teaches that knowledge *is* character. "Fools despise wisdom and instruction" (Prov. 1:7). Studying, reading, memorizing, taking tests, figuring out math problems, presenting speeches, writing papers, recopying papers, and researching are all very difficult jobs that require patience, diligence, endurance, faithfulness, self-denial, and even sometimes courage. This is what character building is all about. We must not buy the propaganda that tells us that academics will not build character. Teaching children to do chores around the house or to be respectful to their classmates and teachers is undoubtedly part of their education. But to neglect academics in favor of these things is entirely unnecessary. I believe it can become a seemingly pious excuse for laziness.

Another common temptation is to assume methods are spiritual by nature. In other words, some Christian writers and teachers will promote their method as the only possible Christian way for parents to educate. I have seen this in homeschool literature where the case is made that to educate outside the home is to compromise spiritually, and I have seen parents whose children are in a private or day school shake their heads with disapproval over the whole concept of homeschooling. When we begin to be imperialistic about our own method, we go beyond God's Word. Not every family is called to homeschool, and not every family is called to the Christian day school. God has made us with different desires, resources, abilities, circumstances, and opportunities. In our church we have families who homeschool, families who use tutorials, families who enroll their children in the private Christian school, and families who use some combination of the three. It is lovely when we can live together in peace and not squabble or quibble over how we differ on our views of education. We will alienate our brothers and sisters in Christ and become spiritually arrogant if we insist that others must agree with us on this. The principle is to educate our children *Christianly.* Families who care deeply about their children's education (and all Christians should) have much in common even if they have made different educational choices.

Some suggest that girls really do not need a rigorous education if they are going to assume the duties of wives and mothers. This view can be seen in the homeschool where the girls drop academics early on, and it can be seen in day schools when parents don't really care if their daughters excel academically, just so long as their sons do. This is very short-sighted and assumes that the men in the Church today do not need wise helpers. Women should be educated as rigorously as possible to prepare them to be women of wisdom and character who will be fine helpmeets for their husbands. If they are called upon to homeschool their own children, they will be prepared to educate their sons and daughters. Uneducated women are not what the Church today needs. Rather, the Church today needs women who are trained to think and act biblically, women who stand head and shoulders above the "career women" of today because they see their education and calling as a means to a very important and significant end. Some may see educated Christian women as a threat to Christian men. They can only be a threat to lazy men, and those men are not the ones who will need well-educated helpmeets.

We must beware of mediocrity, excuses, and laziness. When we excuse ourselves from hard work because we are working on "character," we deceive ourselves. When we do not provide a rigorous education for our daughters because we don't think they'll "need" it, we are short-sighted and may be using this as an excuse for our own laziness. We may also allow laziness to intrude when we allow sentimentality to guide our educational decisions. "He just isn't interested in reading yet, so I'm waiting until he wants to learn." "His teacher is just too hard on him, expecting him to want to read this early." This is not what God created parents to do. Parents must decide when the children should begin learning. It does not much matter whether a child wants to, although it does help considerably to work with a child who has a cooperative attitude. This is what discipline and training are about—Mom and Dad have decided it is time. If we allow our children to persuade us to give in whenever it is hard on them, they will grow up making excuses. Insisting that children turn in their homework to their teachers at school or to Mom at home is one way we can avoid being sentimental and soft. When our son was in fifth grade, his Latin teacher called to tell us he had missed turning in a few assignments. When we talked to him about it, he had done the work but just didn't turn it in. He had left his assignments in his locker and thought that if he had done it, that was enough. This actually became the turning point in my son's academic career because his father made it very clear that such behavior would have some painful short-term consequences. After a very few episodes, the assignments got in on time. He looks back on this as the only thing that kept him from becoming a lazy, do-nothing student.

We must remember as we educate our children that our girls are to be trained to be home-centered, because that is their calling, but our sons should not be home-centered in the same way. Our sons need to be focused outside the home to find their calling. Because of this danger, homeschooling moms must beware of domesticating their sons. Parents with daughters in day schools must be careful their girls do not become career oriented. This is a difficult task when the boys are kept at home all day with Mom, or the daughters are in the school environment, but I have seen both obstacles successfully overcome. Once we know what the potential dangers are, we can take steps to protect both our sons and our daughters.

We must also beware of generalizations. We have all, no doubt, heard disparaging remarks about both dayschoolers and homeschoolers. It is important that we receive criticism with meekness, and do not react in a defensive manner. At the same time, we ought to know when to laugh. Some of the common criticisms I have heard about children in day schools include that they are worldly, give in easily to peer pressure, are uncreative and mechanical, and only know how to relate to their peers. I have also heard homeschoolers criticized as being socially maladroit. In all these criticisms we should look for anything that is helpful and reject the rest. My husband and I have been involved in private Christian education for the past twenty years, and I have seen first-hand examples of all the things suggested above as criticisms. But I have seen them all in both educational systems. I have seen impolite, arrogant children from both backgrounds. When we begin name-calling, we are usually looking for a fight, and that should never motivate us in this issue of education. Parents always make the difference, and it is helpful to know where we need to watch.

We should encourage one another to not grow weary in doing good. Educating our children is a good work that God has prepared in advance for us to walk in. Of course it is hard work. Sometimes it is exhausting work. But parents are required to be engaged in the process and not coasting on cruise control. When my children were little, I helped in their classrooms, on field trips, etc. When they were older, I began to teach in their Christian school, and I taught them all junior-high English and later high-school literature and rhetoric to our youngest. Now that they are in college (and beyond), I proof papers, listen to speeches, and sometimes drill for exams. We must never be done with our involvement in their lives, in their education. And when my grandchildren are old enough to begin their formal schooling, whether at home or enrolled in the Christian school, I pray that I can be an encouragement and help some way. The important thing is to continue to press on, even when our children pass us up; and if we do our job well, they *will* pass us up.

We must never be afraid to reevaluate our options. Some feel it is a sign of failure to go from dayschooling to homeschooling or vice versa. Some think if they change their course, it looks like a defeat. This is not a sign of failure. Indeed, the opposite may be true. You may be rescuing your child from failure. We as parents must not be afraid of peer pressure, what everyone will say about what we do. We do not want our children to be influenced by peer pressure. What about us? Do we want to please the crowd? Are we making our educational decisions based on what others are doing or on what others will say? Are we trying to fit in or impress people by how we educate our children? These are poor reasons indeed to homeschool or to enroll our children in a Christian school. We are accountable to God for how we educate or don't educate our children. We must not spend our time comparing our children to other people's children.

At the same time, we must realize that no perfect education exists. We must be content to give our children the best that we can and not be constantly comparing. If your child is learning math from a certain text and you find that a friend is using something else, don't panic. We can waste a lot of time and money switching curricula, switching schools, switching from one thing to the other. Because of the growing number of wonderful resources, parents can become worried over what to use. We must rest while we work; we must rest in God's care over us as we educate our children. I am convinced that our youngest got a better education in some areas than her older siblings because of the growth of the teachers. But, on the other hand, she missed some wonderful teachers that her brother and sister had. So each child got a different education, and not one was perfect.

Our objective is to develop a culture that loves and promotes learning in a way that honors and glorifies God. Our Christian communities should encourage education, should love and honor learning, and should reflect a reverence and awe for understanding the world that God has made for us. In the context of fearing God, we should pursue knowledge and wisdom and pass on to our children a delight and joy in learning all that we can.

CHAPTER ELEVEN

The Pleasant Home

Go eat your bread with joy. (Eccl. 9:7)

No matter how much teaching we receive about our duties and responsibilities in mothering, it will not have any direct impact on our families if we are simply hearers and not doers of the Word. We can listen to sermons, attend seminars, read books like this, and deceive ourselves into thinking we are actually applying what is taught when in reality we are just talking about it more than we used to. James warns us to beware of such self-deception.

A pleasant home should be full of joy and full of beauty—the beauty of holiness. Though these are closely connected, the first is more important because it is the foundation for the second. There can be no holiness apart from joy-inducing forgiveness and redemption. We must understand that the beauty that accompanies holiness is impossible apart from transforming grace. This beauty sloshes over into our surroundings as we strive to make our homes reflect the goodness, glory, and majesty of God's perfect beauty. We have all seen houses that are superficially "beautiful," but they are full of miserable people. Magazines devote pages and pages to display such homes for us. Unregenerate people look for meaning and fulfillment in "stuff" and that often includes building massive, impressive, impeccable homes. But it obviously does not satisfy the soul-hunger. They know they are hungry, but they do not know where to go to be satisfied. My husband has used an example I love, so I will quote him here. The unbeliever can pile up the cans of peaches, but because he is unregenerate, he does not have the power to open the can and enjoy the peaches. He can stack them up in impressive piles, look at them, count them, imagine he's eating them, but there's no getting at them. The Christian, on the other hand, has the power by God's grace to open the jar and rejoice and delight in the peaches as a precious gift from our merciful Creator. The Christian can *taste* the peaches. The gospel reaches us in our darkness and sinfulness and transforms us into light-loving, light-embracing people.

God's people, of all the people in the world, ought to be a rejoicing people because we, of all people, have much to rejoice about. Our homes should be pleasant, happy, lovely reflections of the joy we have received in Christ. Here is a thought test you can run to see if your home is indeed a pleasant place to be. Is there rejoicing in your "tents"? Does your home spill out sweetness and light? Is it pleasant for the family as well as guests? Do your husband and children look forward to being home? Are you an oasis of comfort to your family when they come home? Is it a peaceful, happy aroma that pervades? Or, on the other hand, is there quarreling, bickering, nagging, criticism, grumpiness, constant correction, and other assorted displays of unhappiness?

Women need to understand the tremendous impact they have on their homes for good or ill. Proverbs tells us that it is better to live in a corner on the roof than in the same house with a contentious woman. Though marriage should be a blessed state, sometimes it is worse than being all alone. The man living in the howling wilderness is better off than the man living with a nagging wife. Most nagging and contention are the fruit of bitterness and a critical spirit. If women would take the time to confess their sins instead of the sins of their husbands, much more fruit would be evident in their lives and homes. Instead of adapting to the status quo of snapping at the children and complaining to the husband, if a wife would seriously undertake to live in a manner worthy of the gospel, the atmosphere in the home would dramatically change. Just as keeping a tidy home requires constant "picking up," so keeping things spiritually tidy requires the same sort of diligence. This means repentance and confession immediately. Putting off confession is just like leaving a kitchen full of dishes to do in the morning. It's no fun getting up to a mess, and it's actually more work when all the food is dried on the plates. Not only that, but the breakfast dishes add to the pile. To keep the atmosphere clear and clean, confession and repentance should take place regularly; it should never be put off, because one sin leads to another, and before you know it, you have a mountain of confessing to do, much like the mountain of dirty dishes in the sink. And you have to attack your sins the same way: one at a time.

Wives must be diligent to study their duties to their husbands and children and to perform their duties cheerfully and patiently. This is not too much to ask, because God always supplies the grace to obey His commands. If things have stacked up, it looks like too much trouble to clean it all up. It may take some time, but you must begin. There are eternal consequences to these things. It is not a simple matter of what *you* like; it is a far weightier matter of what God likes. God requires wives to be respectful and submissive. I have seen many women, who profess to know all about the Bible's teaching on marriage, simply disregard their duties of respect and submission when they feel like it. God does not call us to obedience when we feel like it. We show God that we love Him by obeying His commands. He always provides grace and strength to the one who asks. We must not think we can simply rely on our own steam, for we will run out pretty quickly. We must look to Him who enables. We cannot produce fruit by ourselves anymore than we can cause a child to grow in the womb. God gives the fruit. We work out what He works in. He has prepared good works for us to walk in, and our demeanor in the home is a central part of these good works.

The pleasant home is gracious. This means it is full of grace. If Christ is not present in our lives, He is not present in our homes. We cannot attempt to call Him up to appear whenever we want Him, perhaps during family devotions at dinnertime. We are to serve Him, present our bodies to Him as living sacrifices, every day of our lives. If Christ reigns in our lives, then it follows that He will reign in our homes. This aroma of Christ is what makes our homes more than pleasant. It makes them glorious.

In all, then, a pleasant home is where our families can laugh together, relax together, work together, eat together in harmony and love. It is not a place where our children had better tow the line or Mom will jump on them.

A second test is more visible to the eye. Is your home a lovely place to be? It's not enough to have those magazines with the pictures of lovely homes on your coffee table. Is yours as lovely as you can make it be? Is the table covered with a fresh tablecloth? Is there a flower in the window sill? Do you ever light a candle in the evening? What kind of music is playing? What kind of artwork is on the walls? Is the laundry put away? Are the dishes done? Are the curtains drawn back to let in the day? Does your home smell fresh and sweet? Is it filled with good things? Books, songs, flowers, comfortable corners, family pictures, toys, and more books? Does it often smell of cookies or bread baking? Does your husband come home to the wonderful aroma of dinner coming out of the oven? Or are there unfinished piles scattered about the house, unfolded laundry and dirty dishes, bad smells in the refrigerator and in the bathroom, mold in the corners, beds rumpled and unmade, and toys spread from stem to stern?

A tidy, well-managed home certainly contributes to the pleasantness. But a tidy, fussy home is not pleasant. If the kids can't sit on anything or touch anything, it is far from a relaxing, enjoyable place to be. We want our children to learn good manners, of course, but we want them to love their homes and feel comfortable having friends over to share it.

There will always be things that are "off limits." But there should be far more things and areas where children are welcome. Homes should not be museums or monuments to our good taste. They are to be enjoyed. Like the pretty teacup that never gets used, what is the point of a beautiful room no one can relax in for fear of breaking something or soiling something? We are to enjoy the beauty God has created and be good stewards of it. That means teaching our children how to drink out of the crystal and the good china teacup as well as the tommy-tippee cup.

Some people decorate their homes as though they had bought a paint-by-number kit: the chair sits there, the wall sconces hang on either side of the mirror over the couch, the silk fig tree is plopped in the corner, and the basket of silk flowers sits on the piano, right next to the family photo, and, presto, it's a living room right out of a catalog. This is playing it safe. To fit into this picture, the children (one boy and one girl) are well-dressed and seated sedately on the couch, not touching anything. But this isn't God's picture. His picture is a table with olive shoots all around. A home is not static. It should not look like a picture in a catalog. If we want our homes to have soul, we must pursue God's view of beauty, not necessarily the world's view. Certainly the unbelievers get many things right; this is common grace. But we must get over the idea that we can't decorate by ourselves. Granny's antique rocker, the stool we got at the yard sale, the pillow embroidered by friend, the stack of baby's books, the sheets of music at the piano, the flowers picked from the garden this morning: these are what give our homes soul and make them pleasant to be in. Now I am not here to promote a certain kind of decorating. We all have different likes, opinions, and resources. We put the bowl of fruit on the table because we love the way it lights up when the sun pours in the window. We are God's people. He created light and texture and color for His glory and our delight. The more we delight in His gifts, the more we can please Him.

Our homes are the canvases He has given us to paint. Let us paint them with soul, with gospel, and with all our might.

The pleasant home must be spiritually clean and physically clean. One without the other will be an incomplete picture. God cleans us inside and out. How we are on the outside is a reflection of what we are on the inside. To say that one doesn't matter is to miss the impact of the gospel. To say that how your house looks doesn't matter as long as everyone is happy is like saying the gospel doesn't affect the externals. And that is a sad mistake.

CHAPTER TWELVE

The Domestic Arts

That they may teach the young women to be . . .
keepers at home. (Tit. 2:4-5)

Domesticity is a devotion to home and family life. How few
in our day understand it. But Christian women can embrace
the call to domesticity. This is our territory, and in a sense,
we Christians *own* it. The unbelieving woman cannot experience the fullness of joy there is in being domestic to the
glory of God. The unbeliever can struggle to *do* domestic
things, but she cannot *be* domestic under the blessing of
God. God created marriage, He creates homes, He delegates
the management of the home to the wife, and He gives us
the desire and the ability to imitate Him in "creating" lovely
surroundings for our families in our homes.

The domestic arts are quickly becoming obsolete. How
many women know how to cook anything besides a micro-
wave meal? Women are too busy at the office to bake bread or
to care about preparing meals. There really is no such thing
as a super-mom. She has to make a choice: Will she manage
her home or work at a full-time job outside the home? It is
impossible to do both long-term, and domesticity is a long-
term commitment with long-term benefits and blessings.

Christian wives and mothers must see domesticity as
their duty and calling, not as an option. Whether we turn to
Proverbs 31 or consider what the older women are to teach
the younger women in Titus, it is clear in Scripture that
domesticity is what women are called to and equipped for

since creation. When we embrace our calling, we flourish and find joy in obedience. God does not leave us without direction. He has designed us to perform what He has called us to do, and He gives grace to enable us to obey. Our homes are microcosms which should picture the orderliness of the church, the community, the country. Obviously, a church full of disordered homes will be a disordered church. We must see that what we do in our homes has very important consequences in the church. That should help inspire us to work hard in our homes to make them healthy members in Christ's kingdom on earth.

What are the domestic arts? Besides childrearing, they include cooking, cleaning, sewing, gardening, and decorating. These are the obvious categories. But domesticity also includes many other areas like knitting, refinishing, painting, entertaining, arranging flowers, crocheting or tatting, needlepoint, embroidery, or smocking. Many mothers feel ill-equipped in the big categories like cooking, and they wonder how they can teach their daughters to be domestic while they still don't get it. It is essential that we learn so that we can pass these things on. The glory of the picture in Titus of the older women teaching the younger women is that much wisdom is passed on from generation to generation, preserving important information and helping establish future generations in their callings.

Because the table is a central metaphor for fellowship in the Bible, it is essential that mothers learn how to cook good food and learn how to put it on the table in a beautiful way. Christian women, of all women on earth, ought to glory in beautiful china and crystal and table linens and flower arrangements. Why? Because it is a picture of the fellowship we have at Christ's table. How will His table be set? More lovely than anything we can imagine. Even if you have a very small income, you can set a beautiful table. Make some cloth napkins if you have to (that's a great first sewing project) or find some on sale somewhere. It takes pennies to wash them; paper napkins cost money, and we just throw them away. Gather up vases you can use to bring flowers inside. Buy some cookbooks that will help you learn some simple recipes. And of course, do not be reluctant to ask for help. Perhaps you or your daughters can take some cooking classes from a proficient cook in your church and trade for some babysitting or something. Dinnertime is the most important time of the day. Mother should put some serious time and planning into this daily event. We often underestimate what it takes to put a wonderful meal on the table: it takes planning a menu, shopping for the ingredients, preparing the food, serving it, and cleaning up the mess. To accomplish all this on a regular basis requires some time-management skills. Without some weekly planning and shopping, meals will be thrown together and haphazard.

Next is cleaning. Though it isn't a Bible verse as some think, cleanliness *is* next to godliness. It may sound simple, but there really is much to be learned about cleaning efficiently. Again, Christians of all people should be the cleanest people (body and soul) and have the cleanest homes on earth. Why? Because we have been washed ourselves, and we understand the connection between clean spirits and clean homes. One of the signs of spiritual health in a home is clean floors, clean toilets, clean kitchens, clean sheets, and clean closets. But it also includes clean clothes and clean children. Keeping our homes clean should be as important to us as feeding our families. It is not optional. If your home is dirty, you are teaching your children that clean people should feel comfortable in dirty surroundings, and this is simply not true. A disordered home springs from a disordered soul. Our homes always reflect who we are on the inside. Look around at your home. Is it telling the truth about you? Or is it telling a lie? Get to work and keep your homes clean. That means more than tidy. Tidy is nice, but it isn't necessarily clean. We must keep our families in clean clothes, and we must keep our children clean. This means daily bathing and lots of laundry: washing, ironing, mending, etc. Sending your children (or yourself for that matter) out in sweaters with missing buttons, shirts with stains, or jeans with holes is a sign of poor home management. Designate a mending basket, and don't let anyone wear the clothes in it until they are mended. Little children who are not washed are not loved, because, after all, washing our children is one of the many ways we do love them. God's people should be clean people, inside and out. Of course, the goal is to teach them to wash themselves, mend their own clothes, keep their own rooms clean, and help with the upkeep of the rest of the house. When we clean our homes and all that is in them, we should do it with a consciousness of the correlation between our work of cleaning and God's work of cleaning us. This will help us see the good work we are doing so we will not grow weary in it.

Sewing, gardening, decorating—these are other areas of domesticity where women can take dominion over their homes to the glory of God. But these things are secondary to our home-keeping, cooking, and childrearing. Our daughters are not prepared for marriage if they do not have some experience and expertise in all these areas. Again, older women in the church community are tremendous resources for information in all these and more areas. I have learned many things from the older women in our church. One taught me to can peaches, pickles, applesauce, and pears when my youngest was a baby. Another has taught me much about refinishing, painting, decorating, and planning a wedding. Others have taught me about entertaining and etiquette, gardening, sewing, and cooking. And of course, my own dear mother has taught me the most of all. She enjoys every aspect of homemaking and taught me (and still teaches me) with loving patience to cook (I still have my first cookbook), to sew, to knit, to decorate, etc. She has also taught my girls and her other granddaughters many things in the domestic arts. We should not be so quick to turn to magazines or TV shows for help when we may have a treasure trove of creativity and experience in our mothers or in other women in the church or community. Many of these older women would love to be asked.

I have been urging the college girls in our church to be domestic, and it has been very exciting and gratifying to see the results. My daughter has learned to tat from a ninety-four-year old woman, and she has since taught several of her friends. This art of lacemaking is quickly dying out. At my weekly college girls' study, I have encouraged the girls to bring their handwork. Some are quilting, crocheting, tatting, while others are embroidering. It is quite an impressive group. One of these young ladies commented that it seemed in this community that the more educated the girls become, the more domestic they become. This observation was a great blessing to me, because we don't want our girls to become educated so they will abandon their calling; rather, we want their education to equip them all the more to be domestic.

Mothers have a duty to love domesticity and all it encompasses. We must learn to excel in all these things so that we can teach our daughters as well as younger women in the church to love homemaking.

CHAPTER THIRTEEN

Letting Them Go

Therefore shall a man leave his father and his
mother. (Gen. 2:24)

When the children are little it is very hard, and even a little
sad, to think of them ever leaving our home. But even while
they are small, we must train ourselves to think biblically
about these things. When my son left home to go to graduate
school on the other side of the country, someone asked me
if it was hard to have him gone. I told her that of course it
was hard; I missed him very much. "But," I told her, "there
is one thing worse than a son leaving home, and that is a
son who doesn't."

We want to train and equip our children so that when
they are of age (somewhere after eighteen or so), they will
be able to leave our homes to lead productive, godly lives on
their own. It is not my purpose here to discuss when leaving is appropriate, but I will mention a couple of things in
passing. Some say young men and women should not leave
their parents' homes (under any circumstances) until they
marry. Though this may be ideal for young women, young
men may need to establish their independence sooner, either
for their education or for a job. Young women, if they are still
unmarried in their mid or late twenties, may need to move
out for various reasons. Perhaps they are attending school
or perhaps they are working. Perhaps they want to have the
experience of decorating and managing a home. In either
case, a daughter should remain under her father's authority,

even if she is not under his roof, until she is given in marriage. Because each family has different circumstances, it is impossible to make a rule to cover all the possibilities. The point here is that someday, some way, your children should leave your household and establish their own. This is good and healthy. It is God-ordained. Mothers should not be blind-sided by this. Rather, they should rear their children knowing that the goal is maturity; the objective is to see our children become responsible adults who are no longer under our authority nor under our roof.

The world makes us worry when they refer to the empty-nest syndrome, etc. But we do not live for our children; we live to glorify God. If we have idolized our children and made them central in our lives, then when they leave, we will be aimless and devoid of purpose. Obviously, if we have done our job faithfully in the rearing of them, we will not be afraid to see them mature and leave our nest. We will be excited to see what God is going to do in and through them as He establishes them in new families.

I have heard several mothers tell me how wonderful life still is when their children are all grown. And I can testify, with two out of the three gone, that this is true. It is a great joy and privilege to see your children applying all you have taught them as they study or marry and rear their own children—grandchildren! This is all and more than they say it is. The blessing of grandchildren is inexpressible. Your relationship with your husband, if you have been nurturing it while you've nurtured your children, can continue to grow and flourish. You can enjoy your children as adults and take delight in how God blesses them in their families. You can take on your new role as a support and encouragement as grandparents. It is a beginning, not an end, when your children leave your home under the blessing of God.

Of course every change brings some adjustments, and life is full of changes. You must learn how to take on this support role while letting go of being in charge. If you have been gradually letting go all along as your children get older, this should not be a jolt, but a gentle end of a long process. You may have to learn how to fill time that used to be full of other things. And there is nothing wrong with missing your children when they move out. But you must miss them in the right way, not in a maudlin, self-centered, unbiblical manner.

Sometimes when the children move out, you will be called to begin caring for your own parents. This is right and good. Then the grandchildren can enjoy their great-grandparents, and you can continue to pour yourself out for your family. This is a godly example to your own children of how you want to be cared for when you are in need in your elderly years. Many parents think that when their children are grown, they will really begin living—vacation cruises and no responsibilities to tie them down. This is not the biblical pattern. We are to be fruitful our entire lives, giving ourselves to our families, our church, our community. Retirement may come at sixty-five, but it should not signal the end of productivity. We are to remain fruitful, contributing members of the church community as long as God gives us the capability.

Finally, we must study to be the kind of parents that our children will want to be around when they leave home. If we are domineering, critical, or manipulative, we will drive them away. We want to undertake to be the kind of parents and grandparents who will continue to be a source of great blessing. This may not be as demanding as the full-time parenting of little ones, but it takes great wisdom and humility. The woman who has feared God in her child-rearing does not have to be afraid for the future. "Give her the fruit of her hands; and let her own works praise her in the gates" (Prov. 31:31).

more from Canon Press

The constitution of a biblical home consists of faith, hope, and love, but the greatest of these is love. Love is not to be understood as mere sentiment, but rather self-sacrificing obedience to the Word of God—with a whole heart. This can be quite an elevating and inspiring concept until there are dishes to be done.

In a real sense, the kitchen is near the center of the home, and it's there as a place of *preparation*. It's not a room that exists for itself. In just the same way that clothes were not created for the washing machine, so the food was not destined to end in the kitchen.

What is the kitchen? If you look at it one way, it's a place of endless preparations, punctuated with periods of dealing with the aftermath, by which I mean the cleaning up. But we have to keep in mind *constantly* that the Christian faith sees such service as a form of exaltation. Faith that works in love, as the text above says, is not faith that seeks out the limelight. When we serve one another *in love*, we come to learn that God has designed the world to work in such a way that the majority of the time, we don't get the credit we think we deserve. Self can work hard, but it chafes under the biblical way of working hard. Love gives it away. And when everyone in the family loves—the kind of love you see in a Christian kitchen—the effect is glorious.

My Life for Yours
A Walk Through the Christian Home
Douglas Wilson